Born in 1959 in Hemel Hempstead, Dougie Brimson went directly into the RAF from school where he trained as a mechanical engineer. After serving for over eighteen years and attaining the rank of sergeant, he left the forces in 1994 to pursue a career as a writer. He is married to Tina (a lapsed Hammer) and has three children.

Eddy Brimson was also born in Hemel Hempstead, in 1964, and after leaving school, he trained as a graphic designer. He is married to Harriet, a Gooner!

The Brimsons are the authors of three previous books, *Everywhere We Go*, *England, My England* and *Capital Punishment* – all of which were published by Headline.

# Derby Days

## The Games
## We Love to Hate

Dougie and Eddy Brimson

First published in 1998
by HEADLINE BOOK PUBLISHING

20 19 18 17 16 15 14 13 12 11

ISBN 0 7472 5868 6

Typeset by Avon Dataset Ltd, Bidford-on-Avon, Warks

Printed and bound in Great Britain by
Mackays of Chatham plc, Chatham, Kent

HEADLINE BOOK PUBLISHING
A division of Hodder Headline PLC
338 Euston Road
London NW1 3BH

# Contents

As ever, our thanks go to our long-suffering families, especially our wives, Tina and Harriet. But, primarily, this book is for the down-trodden supporters who walk through a turnstile rather than reach for the remote control.

Keep the faith, lads, and 'Up the 'Ornets'. We beat the scum 4–0, 4/10/97.

# PREFACE
# Setting The Record Straight

Since the publication of our first book, *Everywhere We Go*, many things have been written in the media about the two of us. Some of them have been supportive and encouraging, and some have not. Similarly, we have been lucky enough to receive some blinding reviews of our work in everything from the *Sunday Times* to the *Morning Star*, but we have also had a few that have been far from complimentary. That's life, you can't please everyone and, to be honest, the media perception of us has never really been that much of a concern anyway. We have never made any secret of the fact that our books are written for the genuine and long-suffering football fan rather than those who discovered football after reading *Fever Pitch*. As a result, we place far more importance on the letters we receive and our position in the book charts. They provide us with a far more accurate indication of our achievements.

Yet while we readily accept valid criticism, and concede that some journalists are basically doing what their editors tell them to do rather than actually using their own initiative, it has become apparent that the success of our books seems to rest uneasily with certain hacks at certain magazines. At least two magazines have put forward serious accusations against us and the time has come to set the record straight.

In the summer of 1997, the anti-Fascist magazine, *Fighting*

*Talk*, labelled the two of us as racist. Then, just a few weeks later, that bible of the anally retentive trendy football fan, *When Saturday Comes*, allowed John Williams of Leicester University the space to mount an attack on our books, politics and beliefs which, like the article in *Fighting Talk*, wasn't exactly supportive. To be fair, we slag off academics and their 'studies' (sic) in all our books, but what he did was personal and worse than that, it was wrong. And here's the proof.

Since Eddy was born in 1964, he has, officially, belonged to only three organisations in his entire life; the Watford FC Supporters' Club, the Toyah Wilcox Fan Club (in his defence, he was only 15) and finally, the Anti Nazi League. Dougie, who for the record was born in 1959, has only ever joined one organisation with any kind of political link and that was the Royal Air Force. As an ex-serviceman who took an active part in both the Falklands and Gulf conflicts, Dougie knows full well that the use of violence or intimidation to achieve any kind of ambition, be it political or otherwise, is futile and so he could not give a shit about the extreme right or the extreme left. If that information in itself isn't enough for those who attack us, then they might be interested to read a few other things.

Towards the end of 1996, Dougie spent every spare minute of his time attempting to set up a campaign aimed directly at ridding the game of all forms of intimidation – including physical, abusive and racist. He canvassed support from numerous individuals and organisations including Tony Blair, John Major, Kate Hoey, Tom Pendry, Tony Banks, David Mellor, the FA, the PFA, the ISA network, the FSA (who never responded), UEFA, FIFA, etc. All those who replied pledged support, but not financial assistance. After three months' hard work, a letter arrived from the FA pledging to back the campaign if he could raise the funds. As a result of this deeply disappointing response, Dougie gave up in disgust. Much wiser and about £3000 poorer.

Undaunted, the two of us continued with our quest to force the game to deal with this issue. When the Football Task Force

(FTF) was established, we really believed that we had got somewhere and something would be done. Yet despite numerous letters and faxes to Tony Banks, David Mellor and Rogan Taylor, pleas on the radio and a great deal of pressure, no one ever responded and the call never came. Even when England fans had problems in Rome (as predicted in *England, My England*) and Manchester United fans had problems in Rotterdam, nothing. The tragedy was, as all this was happening, Mellor was all over the media proving just how little he really knows about the issue and we were sat by the phone, desperate to use all our knowledge and experience and play our part.

Despite this, we carried on doing what we could, when we could. When the draw for the first round of the FA Cup in November 1997 pitched Watford with Barnet, we realised that here was another opportunity to do something positive. We immediately contacted both clubs and suggested the idea of a 'Supporters United' day, as a way to involve the fans in the build-up to the game and ensure that the first ever Hertfordshire derby would be played in the best possible spirit. To their eternal credit, both Barnet and Watford thought it was a great idea and grabbed it with both hands. As a result, with their support and active participation, a series of events were arranged between the two sets of fans to give them the opportunity to build a friendly relationship rather than the more usual hostile one between local rivals. These events included two football games between groups of supporters, and even a penalty shoot-out on the pitch at half-time between the two fanzines. Not only that, but thanks to the efforts of everyone involved, the actual match day was one big party for the supporters and it was a huge success. Maybe those who condemn us might see this as proof that the will to change things really is there. All it took was a little work on our part, and a great deal of work and enthusiasm from others.

However, since we began writing, we have learnt that some people can't avoid criticising others; even when someone does something positive they appear to resent it, perhaps because they didn't think of it first. With the two of us, the main thrust of the attack has been aimed at our stance on racism. At the risk of becoming boring – and apologies to all those with a working brain at their disposal – we must go over it once again.

We have gone on record as saying that we feel the 'Kick Racism out of Football' campaign has become outdated to such an extent that it is now in great danger of becoming counter-productive. Our reason for saying this is simply that, while we readily and happily acknowledge that the campaign has achieved a great deal in its time, it has been done to death and the average supporter has become almost immune to the anti-racism message. When people get bored of something, they take no notice of it. You can relaunch it with new packaging, a new name and even new faces as many times as you like, but by then no one will care. However, rather than just slag things off, which is the easy part, we have also put forward a simple alternative proposal: turn the whole thing around. Focus on the success of black and foreign players, show the white kids wearing their Andy Cole shirts and the black kids wearing their Alan Shearer shirts and then tell everyone outside football that this is what we can achieve if we put our minds to it. Yes, of course there are racists who go to football, but there are racists who go to the cinema or visit the British Museum. The difference with football is that, because of the success of 'Kick Racism' in the past and the performance of black players on the pitch, people will turn round to those who chant racist abuse and tell them face-to-face to shut the fuck up, or else they will ask the stewards to do something about it. You may not agree with our suggestions, and that's your prerogative, but disagreeing with 'Kick Racism' now does not make us racist.

Furthermore, in *When Saturday Comes*, John Williams accused us of not including a single 'black voice' in any of our books, but he has no evidence to support this and he is wrong. We know that there are accounts from black and Asian supporters included in our books, because we actually met and interviewed them. There may be others that we don't know

4

about because, as yet, we haven't been able to work out the colour of someone's skin from the way they write a letter. We never mention the colour of someone's skin because it has no relevance and is not an issue with us at all. To do so would merely smack of tokenism.

We made the decision early on that we would be honest in our writing, in the views we express and most importantly honest to ourselves. We believe in every single word we write and will answer any criticism levelled at us be it in a letter – and we are confident enough to put our address at the back of every book – or in a radio or television studio. If we think someone, be they a player, a journalist or an administrator, is a wanker, then we will say so. We will say so not because we have any kind of grudge against them, but because they have provided us with all the evidence to form that opinion. If you go around with not just a chip but a whole bag of spuds on your shoulder and behave like a wanker week in week out then eventually, that will begin to shine through. Your own supporters may not be able to get to grips with that, but you can't fool the rest of us. However, we have found that the hard truth is something many people find difficult to deal with.

If you write something in any kind of publication, be it a book, a Sunday supplement or a club fanzine, you have a responsibility to check your facts before the piece makes it into print because if it is wrong, then once it's published, it is too late. Mud sticks and the effects can linger for a long, long time. But some realise the power at their disposal and what an awesome weapon it is.

By branding us as racist in *Fighting Talk* or hinting that we have certain beliefs in *When Saturday Comes*, these people have thrown mud at us. Whether or not that was the intention, we hope they will now do their utmost to put the record straight. We have proved where our sympathies lie through both our anti-hooligan work and our writing: with the football supporter. We don't care if they're black, white, Asian, Christian, Jewish, vegetarian, heterosexual, lesbian or even from Manchester. By now, everyone who reads our work, or has met us, should know exactly which direction we are coming from.

# Introduction

We have often been heard to remark that being a football fan is akin to having an addiction. Indeed it is fair to say that we have written thousands of words on the obsessional behaviour of supporters and the things that make them, and us, tick. It may be stating the obvious, but there is no doubt that being a true football fan involves much, much more than taking passing glances at the back pages or slobbing in an armchair while watching teletext or Sky Sports.

That is the easy way and we could all do that if we so desired. But that isn't our way because, for us, and all those who watch their football in the flesh, football is about being there. Walking out the front door with your ticket in your pocket is part of the whole thing, just as important as the noise, the smells, the weather and the pre-match pint. Football is an occasion, an event to be enjoyed no matter what your team or where you watch them, be it Goodison Park or the local park.

The beauty of football is that it is always changing. No game is the same as the last one and no journey the same as previous ones. Every time we pass through those turnstiles to gaze across the green expanse, we know that the game we are about to see could be *the* game, the one we've been waiting for and dreaming about when everything clicks and a footballing lesson is administered. In truth, for the vast majority of football fans who watch their football at grounds other than Highbury, Old Trafford or Anfield, the chances are that it won't be, but we live in hope because we know, we just know, that one day...

Of course, at the end of the season, when our teams have let us down (again), destroyed all our hopes and failed to make the play-offs (again), have been relegated (again) or have spent the entire season merely making up the numbers, we can be safe in the knowledge that come August, we will all once again, be equal. Every club, even those struggling to survive, will have the same opportunity to shine as everyone else. This coming one could be the season, the championship maybe, even a long cup run? Yes, this season for sure. It just has to happen this time. We all have those dreams, and this is the time to have them, because we know that there are only two cups, one championship and various promotion or European places up for grabs. There are plenty of teams fighting for them, and if we were brutally honest with ourselves, we could have a good bet on where most of them will end up. But at the start, we're all equal and the optimism, the hopes and the dreams are positively concrete, fuelled by good old blind faith.

Yet before that start, there is the black hole of the close season. The dreaded time when there is no football and Saturdays become filled with shopping, DIY and gardening. But like all true football fans who languish in that pit of despair, we are aware that there is a light at the end of the tunnel and it is the one thing that wrenches us out of that despairing monotony: the release of the fixture lists.

When the lists for the coming season get published, it is a sign that football is coming. A time when we, as true fans, will be able to walk back into our spiritual home and meet with the people who have shared our elation and gloom for countless seasons. We will welcome them with open arms and hearts just as they will welcome us. That common bond of football fandom is never stronger than at the start of the season when we're all up there, ready and waiting with hope and anticipation like a tightly coiled spring. The first home game, the first away trip, it's all a part of it and it's the dogs' bollocks. Eddy explains:

## YOU WON'T GET THAT ON PAY-PER-VIEW

On Tuesday 2 September 1997 I travelled down from Hertfordshire to watch the Hornets play Plymouth Argyle in a Second Division fixture. Now that's a fair old trek for a midweek match, but I'd never been to Home Park before and the thought of ticking off my 75th English league ground did play a part in my decision to travel down.

I remember coming across two coach-loads of Argyle fans many years ago at a service station up north, they were on their way home from Chesterfield and I remember thinking, 'Fuck me that's a long way.' Then I realised that every away game is a long way for those lads and I've always had a soft spot for Argyle ever since. Dougie and I met some of their lads in Trafalgar Square during Euro 96 and they were tops; true fans with a real passion for their club.

Unfortunately, I had to make the journey down on the club coaches with only myself for company. I must admit that the sight of an old woman carefully placing various knitted mascots and toy Harry Hornets along the front window of the coach very nearly made me head back off to the ticket office asking for a refund but I persevered and took up my seat. As you can imagine, Dougie and I are not the two most welcome people at Vicarage Road these days and, as every other seat was taken, I found myself to be the only lone traveller, the only Billy No-mates on the bus. Still fuck 'em, I wipe my arse on Harry the Hornet. By the time the coach had hit the M4 it had become apparent that the video on this 'executive' bus was never going to work and so long lingering looks out of the window were all life had to offer my next five hours on this planet.

Finally we arrived at Home Park and, after getting the chips in from the local Chinese, I made my way into the ground to be met by a wondrous sight. Home Park is a truly fantastic stadium, a shrine to all that is football and I defy any supporter that has even stood on those terraces to disagree. As the rest of us are forced to sit on plastic seats, in characterless stadiums and surrounded by people we can't move away from, the supporters of Plymouth Argyle FC have Home Park, the BASTARDS.

Within minutes I secure myself a lift home, away from Harry Hornet and his adopted parents, then the rain starts to fall. The teams appear and the lads start brightly. The conversation begins to flow. 'We're taking the piss here. We're going to piss this division.' Then the home side get on top. 'We're shit. They're all over us for fuck sake. Come on you wankers. If you don't win at places like this you don't deserve to get promoted.' Half time comes and it's 0–0; that'll do. The rain gets worse and the coffee is only warm, but would I want to be anywhere else?

In the second half the lads are shooting towards us but most of the game is played in the other half. 'I'd have settled for a point before the game, wouldn't you? Oh yeah. A point here is a good result.' The referee then gives the Hornets a free kick just outside the box. There are 71 minutes on the clock. In comes the shot and the keeper makes a tremendous save. The ball is then laid back to 17-year-old Gifton Noel-Williams who cracks his shot into the back of the net. Gifton I love you. Every one of the 300 Watford fans present goes mad, mental, stupid. I run across the terrace and down to the fence like a man possessed as do all those fellow 'ornets. I give the old finger to the lads of the Central Element who are sitting to our right, (although thankfully they can not see me) and I call the rest of the world a wanker because I am a winner and the lads are 1–0 up.

Please God. Please God! The longest 19 minutes of my life follow. My friend kids himself that a point would still be a good result as Argyle pile on the pressure and then the whistle goes. The Lord has fallen for my prayers, it's 1–0 to the Golden Boys. 'We took the piss and it should have been more really.' Like fuck. Then I remember the walk back to the car park and realise that the locals won't be that happy. I hope the rain and the fact that we have no mob will put them off, but with not a copper in sight it's head down. A few Mums and Dads get pushed and one scarf man gets kicked but we make the safety of the car untouched. 'Yes, yes, YES, 1 fucking 0.' The radio is on in a flash. Bournemouth could only draw and so the Hornets are top of the league. Yes, YES, YES. L*t*n have lost at home 2–0. YES, YES, YES, YES, YES. If Madonna was to now tap on the window and offer horizontal refreshment then on returning home I would have to place my head in the oven and turn it to gas mark 8, because life could never get any better than this.

Then I remember a similar night back in 1981 when we won 1–0 in a midweek game at Wrexham giving a similar outcome, Luther's two goals at Old Trafford, 3–2 at Torquay on Boxing Day. In fact there have been a fair few nights like this when I think about it, that is why *we* go. Supporting your football club in the flesh is great, fucking GREAT.

On the journey home we listen to the results every half hour. 'And Graham Taylor's Watford go back to the top of Division Two following a 1–0 win at Plymouth,' says the presenter. 'We are top of the league, I said we are top of the league' we sing. At 2.00am I arrive home shagged out, I have to be up in five hours.

I write this story for these reasons. I write it to tell all those who follow their football from their front rooms that they will never experience such a feeling unless they get up off their fat arses and follow a team in the flesh. I write this to tell all those that wear the shirt of a team that play 100 miles or more away from where they live, without ever actually going to watch them live to go down and support their local club. I write to tell all those 'experts' on television and in the media that those outside the top flight care as much as anyone else. Finally, I write this to ask all the neo-trendy, celebrity, TV, comedy, music and film star fans that have suddenly appeared if they would ever make a similar journey in support of their team? I doubt it.

Would I have wanted to have been anywhere else? Would I fuck! Up the 'ornets and up true football fans from Land's End to John o' Groats, you know who you are.

People who sit at home and watch games on television do not understand this of course. For them, everything is mapped out to fit in around the latest soap. Even if they miss a game live, they can tape it and watch it later so it doesn't really matter. For most of them, it hardly matters who they're even watching. As long as there's a few goals, a bit of skill or the odd bit of controversy so that Andy Gray or Alan Hansen has got something to prattle on about between adverts. They can sit there in their freshly ironed replica shirts and talk parrot fashion about the skill of Beckham or the marvel that is Le Tissier because they've seen them all from the comfort of their front room and they think that they're fans, as good as us. No, better than us because they support winners and just because they watch them from home makes no difference. It makes them no less a football fan, it doesn't really matter.

But it does matter. It matters to us. The true fans who suffer the high prices and crap weather to see our lads in the flesh, enjoy the atmosphere and watch the game without some half-wit telling us who is on the ball at that precise moment. We know that. We should fucking well know that because we watch it every week and we shout at those players who wear our shirts and who play for us. That's football, that's what it really means and the fixture list is the sign that it is starting again. Not just for Newcastle, Everton or Chelsea but for Macclesfield, Hednesford and Barnet. Every bit as important and every bit as exciting.

Of course the other thing that the fixture lists mean is that we can begin to plan *our* season. The long away trips, the all-ticket affairs and the cup games with the possibility of mid-week replays. We can begin to plan our time off work, our shift patterns and our sick days to make sure that we can get the time off should we need it. Even weddings have to fit in. After all, who in their right mind would want to walk up the aisle when the boys are at home? Not just because of the fact that you'd miss the game but because you know that the lads wouldn't! And let's be honest here, June is a good time to check up on the elderly relatives to make sure that they're all right and of course, May has to be kept clear. Just in case.

For the 'geezers', the arrival of the list means other things. Trips to clubs with serious reputations or visits from firms with scores to settle. New places to go and new foes to encounter. It may not be palatable for some but that's the reality, just another part of the culture and all part of being a fan. Deny it till you're blue in the face but you know we're right. Tell me with a straight face that one of the first fixtures the fans of teams in the Second Division did not look for was the dreaded away trip to the New Den.

While every game has some degree of importance, within those lists lie fixtures that are more significant than others. Games that mean everything and for which the phrase 'I don't give a shit what happens this year, but we have to beat those bastards!' was invented. The local derby.

It would be a complete waste of time even attempting to explain the significance of a local derby to anyone who has to ask. If they don't know, if you don't know, then you're wasting your time reading this book because this book is all about those games. It is about the passion, the humour and, yes the hatred but above all it is about the importance. Football *is* important but for many of us, the local derby is even more important. It means so much and, at times, it means too much.

To those who don't really understand football, there are of course only a few 'real' derby games: the Merseyside affair, the North London giants, Glasgow's Old Firm battle and, on those very rare occasions, the Manchester conflict. You may scoff, but some people genuinely believe that and even the BBC seem to take the line that these games are the only true local affairs. We, as fans, know that this is all bollocks of course. We all have derby rivals, and they are just as important to us and we are just as passionate. Yes, the Merseyside derby is important and the Old Firm clash is a passionate and frenzied affair, but travel over to Suffolk when Norwich play Ipswich or visit Bristol when City meet Rovers and you will experience games that are every bit as intense and every bit as volatile as Spurs versus Arsenal ever was. Just because they are not battling for the top spot in the Premiership doesn't make them any less worthy. Indeed, it is fair to say that the majority of the more inflammatory fixtures are well outside the top flight. It is also fair to say that most games involving local rivals tend to be close fought but often poorly played affairs, because not only are most players aware of the importance of the games to the fans, they know only too well that a costly mistake will almost certainly haunt them forever. Supporters have long memories at the best of times but to be the cause of twelve months' humiliation must be almost too much to bear.

And that is the bottom line really. The local derby isn't just about football. It's about pride and being able to hold your head up when you go to work on the Monday morning or walk through the town centre in your team shirt. It's about satisfaction. Knowing that your lads are as good as, if not better than, the other lot and that you follow the best. Sadly, the opposite is also true. Knowing that your team are shit, the club up the road are better (for now at least) and that ultimately, maybe, you got it wrong and if you had a choice when starting out on the rocky road of football fandom, you chose the wrong colours to follow. If that's the case, then you have to grin and bear it for you have no other option. But you know that when things are turned around, you will revel in the victory knowing full well that any team is only as good as the last result. You have to think like that if your team are shit because otherwise you may as well pack it all in right now.

As Watford fans, of course, we know all this because derby games were, until 4 October 1997, a complete and utter fucking nightmare for us. It's bad enough being forced to let the pox-ridden, sub-human inadequates who watch them into *our* superb home while we're forced to trek up the M1 to pay them money to enter what is without doubt the worst ground in our division, if not the league. But once we were in, at least up until 4 October 1997, we had to put up with the constant references to the fact that we hadn't beaten them for year after year, and it hurt. Bad. Not only did we never beat those scummiest of bastards who happen to be our local rivals, but the truth of the matter is that because we didn't beat them for so long, even a draw was greeted like a win. For us long-suffering Hornets, that was a pain of almost heart-rending proportions. We're not making excuses, but if you look at the history of this fixture, it will show conclusively that in the week before this most important of games, everything always went wrong for us and everything went right for them. We had players who got injured or who started suspensions that week while they had players back from injury or who finished suspensions. We're not making it up, honestly, that's the way it was and it was a pain in the arse.

But all that changed on 4 October 1997, a day that will go down in the history of Watford Football Club and that will live long in the hearts of all those who were there. For once, everything changed. We had a full-strength team out, they had an injury list that no Watford fan could have dreamed for. They were absolutely crap and we were dynamite and, as a result, the Golden Boys dealt out a humiliation of such magnitude, it was almost embarrassing: 4–0. Not only that, but those four goals took just 27 glorious minutes! We ran those fuckers ragged and how we loved it and how we celebrated. Well, after all, if you had waited ten years for something wouldn't you jump around a bit when it came? Of course you would!

It would be tempting fate to say that maybe the jinx has been broken, but as Watford fans we needed that win like we have never needed anything. And we want another one. Local derbies, fucking great!

# PART ONE
# Derby Days

---

# Chapter 1
# The Training

As fans, we take our dislike of our local rivals for granted. It is something we have grown up with and, in a perverse kind of way, learnt to love. After all, a little hatred is a healthy thing and when times are bad, we can blame everything on the scum up the road. Similarly, if you are lucky enough to support a team who regularly stuff their neighbours, then a minute's simple reflection on that last thrashing dealt out by your boys will do wonders for your mood.

To the outsider, it may seem odd that we reflect on life in this way, but as fans, we're all used to these little foibles. We accept them as a natural part of our supporting life and are, to be perfectly honest, happy that they are there.

The new-breeds and the armchair fans cannot get to grips with the concept of this hatred because like most things involved with football-supporting, it is totally irrational. The argument that as citizens we should support *all* our local football sides is, on the face of it, a pretty sound one. But in the real world, for the regular supporter, that idea will never hold sway; the whole concept is almost alien. At Watford, the biggest cheer of the day is at half-time when we hear that the scum are losing – and it's the same at every ground we've ever been to. We want our lads to win, of course, but by fuck we want *them* to lose. It makes our day. Feelings and emotions of this depth do not, obviously, happen overnight. It takes a lifetime to learn to loathe another club to such a level that it becomes second nature.

In most cases, your football allegiances (and dislikes) will have been decided before you were born. If your dad was Liverpool, Man City or Hereford United, so were you. If your dad wasn't a footie fan, then it was your mates you followed. If they were all Arsenal, that was the way you went. It isn't always like that, of course. There are plenty of ways to choose your team, as we all know, but for the most part you followed either your old man, the pack or your local side. If you were lucky, all three might be the same and you would be spared the agony of choosing a team of your own.

As for the two of us, our arrival at our local club came via two different routes. Eddy's choice was determined by the fact that the Hornets were local and his mates went there, while Dougie started at Stamford Bridge before gradually surrendering to the pull of Vicarage Road! However, it should not have been like this at all. As we have mentioned in previous books, our old man is Tottenham through and through and as such, in the natural course of events, we should be regulars down at White Hart Lane. Tragically for him, we rebelled and chose our own way. This meant, for example, that his traditional dislike of Arsenal never filtered down to us. (Indeed, if the truth be known, the opposite is true. We actually dislike Spurs more than the Gunners because it winds him up!) But it also meant that we had to learn to dislike the L*t*n scum and their inbred supporters, for it did not come naturally.

For most fans, the playground provides the first real experience of football rivalry. Some may already have spent their formative years being bombarded with subliminal messages by their dad – such as, 'I'm not going in that sports shop because they sell the scum kit' or 'Look over there, it's a bloody scummer in our town!' – and will be aware of what is expected of them. But in the playground, when the lunchtime games are in full swing, the real impact of local rivalry can be felt for the first time. David from Birmingham tells his tale:

## AT SCHOOL IN BRUM

At my school, you were either Blues or Villa. Nothing else. No Man United, Liverpool or any of that shit. Blues or Villa. At break times, the games were split into obvious sides and they were mental.

We made them worse because we had this thing where we chose a player and stuck with him, so you had about ten mini-versions of Trevor Francis on the Blues side, which made them quite funny as well.

At least once a week they ended up in a fight and then we'd all be banned from playing at break times, but that never lasted more than a day because we all used to hang about outside the offices moaning. We knew that in the end they'd send us out with a ball, just for a bit of peace and quiet. Fucking great times, they were, and I'll tell you what, all those lads are *still* Blues or Villa. It's fucking tragic now, all these little fuckers with their United shirts. Fucking tragic.

Once we leave the sanctuary of school, these feelings are taken into the workplace, where they manifest themselves in other ways. After all, who in their right mind would want to work for a supporter of their local rivals, with all the possibilities for humiliation and retribution that go with it? On the other hand, imagine having people working for you who follow the enemy! The sheer bliss of sending someone to some shithole of a job on the Monday morning after your lads have suffered another defeat. Thankfully, Dougie has some experience of this as for some time, shortly after we finished our first book, *Everywhere We Go*, he spent some time running a department at an engineering company in L*t*n. All the lads who worked for him were scummers and, by all accounts, he made their life a misery. Long trips and even longer hours were the norm if Watford had lost on the Saturday, and if the scum were at home in midweek, overtime suddenly became a necessity. It was a happy time for him. The screensaver on his office

21

computer alternated between 'Up the 'Ornets!' and 'Scum-scum-scum . . .' while their obvious dislike of the Golden Boys was turned to his advantage simply by giving all the dirtiest jobs to those who were the most vocal.

However, Dougie is the first to admit that with the first derby of the season imminent, he lost his bottle and resigned. Like most Hornets, he knew we wouldn't win (well, you do, don't you?) and the thought of walking into work on the back of a defeat, with all that sniggering . . . well, he just couldn't have done it.

Dougie's experience is far from unique. We were once told of a company in Southampton where the top man was a full-bore Geordie and manic Newcastle fan. After a while, he found out that one of his workers was a Sunderland fan and sacked him on the spot, with the comment: 'I'd rather close this factory down than have a Red bastard working for me!' The Roker (or should that be Stadium of Light?) lad stormed into his office, resigned and shouted that he'd rather be on the dole than work for a Geordie! A bit extreme, maybe, but perfectly understandable to some.

It isn't just at work that this distrust is harboured, either. Personally, the two of us have no qualms whatsoever about refusing to have scummers in our homes, and to this end, just inside Dougie's front door is a small plaque with the immortal phrase 'Watford Fans Only' in black and yellow. Anyone who comes to his house is quizzed as to their allegiance and refused entry, sometimes even politely, if they follow the enemy. His children's friends also come under scrutiny and, by now, most of them are well aware of his 'house rules'.

For the two of us, dealing with fans of the scum in this way isn't a problem. It is fairly obvious that they feel the same about us. We doubt whether a book-signing session in the L*t*n Arndale would be an entirely cordial occasion!

For the hooligan groups, this kind of rivalry is even more intense because of the violence associated with it. Not only is there the protection of their patch, manor or reputation to consider, but also the history between the two sets of fans.

Take, for example, the rivalry between Millwall and West Ham. On the face of it, this revolves around the fact that they are both East End clubs, but that is only a part of it. The murder of a Millwall fan at New Cross station in 1976, West Ham ambushing Millwall with firebombs at London Bridge tube station in 1983, the list goes on and on. We focused on the activities surrounding both these clubs' firms in *Capital Punishment*, but the background provided to us here by Cliff shows just how out of hand things can get.

## DOWN IN THE EAST END

The chant 'We hate Cockneys and we hate Cockneys' will often be heard ringing in the ears of both West Ham and Millwall fans many times during a season, but no one hates them more than the two sets of fans hate each other. The north-south divide may bring the lads from other firms together when they are away on their travels, but the thin strip of Thames that separates these two may as well be as wide as an ocean as far as they are concerned. Both sets of fans consider the other side of the river to be a no-go area, and with good reason.

Millwall fans think that the 'Irons' are living on past glories and ignore the fact that their 'yo-yo' existence is testament to a team that like to consider themselves better than they have actually ever been. For West Ham fans, the 'Lions' are simply the lowest of the low, planted firmly in an area that even the rats think of cleaning up before they settle in.

The trouble between the two sets of fans goes back a long way, but there are a few incidents that have fuelled the hatred into a burning furnace. In the 1970s, when both firms were at their most active and dangerous, Millwall appeared to have stolen the limelight by being made the subject of a now legendary television documentary. The programme featured amusingly titled charmers such as Harry the Dog, the F-Troop, the Half-Way Liners and the

surgically-masked lads known as 'Treatment'. Despite the
fact that many of the characters had been made up for
the benefit of the unsuspecting camera crew, they sent a
chilling message into the living rooms of the south east,
as organised groups of football hooligans appeared for
the first time. The fact that Millwall were now seen to be
at the forefront of such activity made the West Ham lads
from across the river just a little bit unhappy, to say the
least.

For those involved in football violence, there is only
one way to prove yourself and that is by taking on the
opposition head-to-head. The West Ham fans didn't take
long in staking their claim of being the top lads in London,
and they did so in the most tragic circumstances. Fate
dictated that Millwall would be playing at home on the
same night that West Ham were paying a visit to nearby
Charlton Athletic. Following a clash between the two rival
groups at New Cross station, a young Millwall fan was
found dead on the tracks. In his hand was a West Ham
scarf. The police, who, like most others, had been taken
completely by surprise by the clash, suggested that he
had stolen the scarf from a West Ham supporter and then
accidentally jumped out of the train on the wrong side
and onto the live rail. His family insisted that he was not
a thug and must have been thrown out of the carriage
onto the rails by West Ham fans, and had grabbed the
scarf as he tried to stop himself falling. The truth was
never revealed, but the rumours were rife and the hatred
between the two sets of supporters grew. Especially
among those that took their support to a more disturbing
level.

A nightmare scenario appeared for the police soon
after, when West Ham were relegated down to the same
division as Millwall, meaning the two would clash twice
in just one season. Headlines such as 'War Feared in Game
of Hatred' were used in the build-up to the first meeting
at Upton Park. It was also reported that leaflets bearing

a photograph of the dead Millwall fan had been circulating in pubs throughout south London. This leaflet urged all Millwall fans to turn out, as this was to be 'no ordinary ruck' and a 'revenge attack we've waited two years for' had been planned. On the day, hundreds of police with dogs and horses were on duty. A helicopter flew overhead – very rare in those days – and the streets were ringed with riot vans and meat wagons, creating a siege-type atmosphere that even the East End found oppressive. Despite such a presence, trouble flared in the sidestreets around the stadium and down in the tube network, forcing many to turn back and wait for the result on the news. The game was poorly attended.

Indeed, the media build-up to the game was, on reflection, almost understandable. The array of weaponry shown on the news the following evening could have supplied a small army: baseball bats, wheel-braces, crowbars, darts; you name it, it was there for all to see. If the media campaign saved just one fan from suffering the result of being on the end of that little lot, then it has to be said that it was justified.

If the events of that night were bad, then the return fixture at The Den was even worse. It appeared that every male between the ages of 15 and 50 living in the East End had made the journey to Millwall.

There must have been a policeman every 10 yards along the Old Kent Road, and at every junction they stood shoulder-to-shoulder. The sight of riot vans flying in all directions, with their sirens blaring, suggested that trouble was never far away. On entering the ground, it became clear that many had stories to tell; some won, some clearly lost. During the walk back to the station, one attack of bottles and bricks from the darkness very nearly saw the police lose control. Most were running for cover, but many were running to battle.

Fortunately for the Met Police, the two sides have generally been kept apart due to their differing levels of 'success' on the pitch, but it is clear that the hatred between the supporters is still there. Let's hope that those levels of 'success' continue, for all our sakes.

Pathetic as it may seem to the outsider, to many supporters those incidents are as much a part of history as the results of the actual games. They form an integral part of a culture that quite simply runs too deep to be forgotten, and which the game ignores at its peril.

# Chapter 2

# Players – The Enemy Within?

As the big guns of the PFA mingle at the Premier League Players' Golf Event, rubbing shoulders with their sponsors, agents, financial advisers, personal drivers, minders and even travel agents, we sometimes ask ourselves if the high flyers within the British game understand just what the derby fixture means to the average supporter anymore. Do they get it at all?

For all of us poor souls following a club deep down in the pants of what remains the Football League, the derby fixture remains all-important. It is a gift, a realistic glimmer of hope in what will be another season of thoughtless football against equally thoughtless sides. Our side will battle to get promoted, only to get relegated again the following season. For this is the real world of penniless, lower league football, yet in a strange way, it has something the top dogs lack: loyalty.

In the good old days, your local side consisted of local lads. The build-up to the derby not only involved them, it positively revolved around them. In the workplace and the pub, all the talk was about 'the game' and that build-up affected everyone. Especially the players, who knew exactly what it meant and how important it was. Sadly, it seems that within the professional game, certainly at the top end, those days have gone.

In some ways, that is understandable. Regrettable, but understandable. As fans, we accept that like most of us, players have to secure a comfortable future for themselves and their families, and we don't begrudge them that one bit. But surely they must have been supporters at some time, and therefore must know that there are certain things you can do and others that you mustn't?

The big wages currently being paid to players have forced them – or enabled them – to live well away from the madding crowd. As a result, they have inadvertently isolated themselves from the average man or woman on the street. You won't often find a top player living at the end of your road these days, because envy has led to their windows or sports cars being smashed to bits (ask Ian Walker). So they are now almost untouchable, unapproachable. But they probably don't realise that not all of that envy is about the fact that they're wealthy. It's about what they do and, in most cases, who they do it for.

The inevitable result of this isolation is that almost the only people players come into contact with are other players, or people who hold them in awe for who and what they are. We used to think that *Coronation Street* appeared before our eyes once too often during the week, but now there seems to be a new programme appearing with almost the same regularity: 'Sports bar opening of the week', featuring the cast of the Premier League and Lancaster Gate. Whenever this programme – or anything of its type – appears, it worries us that everyone seems to know everyone else and that they all get on so well. This, in turn, begs the key question: do they like each other too much for when the big game comes around? They will stand there, arms around each other like an imitation chorus line, and sing each other's praises – just in case their agents are fixing something up in the back of the Jag that may have them playing alongside each other in a matter of weeks. Players may now live next door to each other, yet play for bitter rivals. They will go clubbing or play golf with their man-marker on a Saturday night. And wouldn't it be quite difficult to ask for the return of the lawnmower or another beer if you had been kicking lumps out of your next door neighbour during that afternoon's derby match?

Up at the top, it's got way too pally for our liking. Maybe we've got it wrong and football is only entertainment now, like the cinema or the theatre, and for these lads it's only a job. But to us, football *isn't* like that and the derby match isn't like that at all. Just go into any local on the night of a defeat against 'them' and you'll see what we mean.

Not all players are like that, of course. Take Stan Collymore as an example. He has always had a burning desire to play for the team he has supported since childhood and this is a quality that, as fans, we can't help but admire. Even when playing for Liverpool, one of the biggest names in world football, Stan never made a secret of his support for Aston Villa and openly admitted that the dream move for him would be to Villa Park.

Although he is paid more in a week or two than most of us are in a year, he is happiest because he is banging the goals in for the team he stood and watched when he was a kid, helping the club he supports gain success. For all of us in the stands and on the terraces, that would be our ultimate dream too, and in an era when for players, club loyalty means nothing, Stan shines out like a beacon, in the same way that Steve Bull shines out at Wolves. When the derby fixture comes around, it is only players such as these who understand the mood in the stadium. They will feel the glory or the pain that the result brings to the heart, because to them it's not just another game, not just another win bonus to fight for. It's much more than that.

But Stan, and Steve and those others who can hold their heads up when they use the word 'loyal', are sadly all too rare. There are far too many players who happily ply their trade at other clubs while their own, and by that we mean the clubs where they started to watch the game, almost go to the wall. Did those players who grew up watching their football at the Goldstone Ground feel the same when the club almost folded as those who actually pay at the turnstiles? Maybe, but what did they do about it? Did they offer support, or make a donation to the supporters' groups? We'll never know, of course; maybe some did. But if there is any justice, a few players will have felt the odd pang of guilt when they saw thousands of supporters from every club in the country trying to save one of their own from extinction.

Yet while to a degree this is the acceptable and understandable side of the journeyman player, there are times when a player just should not be playing for a particular side, under any circumstances. Take Robbie Fowler, for instance. Robbie has always admitted to the fact that he supports Everton. So we can't understand how he can pull on a Liverpool shirt every week. The club he claims to love with a passion have suffered in the past few seasons from the lack of firepower up front, while Robbie merrily bangs in the goals for his spiritual enemy! Liverpool supporters have been able to take the piss out of their rivals year after year thanks in no small part to Mr Fowler. If young Robbie had decided to wear the Blue he claims to love so much rather than the Red, things might just be different in that city.

Then you get someone like Chris Waddle – Sunderland till he dies, apparently. Chris used to work in a sausage factory, a place obviously devoid of football fans because he went off to play for Newcastle, giving them some of his best years while Sunderland – his love, remember – struggled to play shit. Ah, but he returned to play for the club he loves so much in his twilight years. Well, isn't that nice for him? Did they really fall for that up there?

The influx of foreign players up at the top has only added to this lack of understanding of the game's emotions. Do you really want a player turning out for you who has a clause in his contract enabling him to jump ship should the team get relegated, leaving you to suffer the consequences? Is that the type of player you can count on if you fall 2–0 behind to your local rivals? Is it bollocks. For him, it's just another match, another 10, 20 or 30 thousand pounds in the bank that week. These players can't hope to understand the culture, the traditions and the expectations of the supporters they are representing – it's just not in their blood. Half the time they seem to be more interested in securing endorsements than points, and that's a kick in the teeth for all those who stand, or sit, watching them. I'd rather have the bloke in the seat next to me wearing the shirt. At least he'd run his heart out for us.

At Watford, we have no such stars to yearn for. For Watford, as we have said on many occasions, are cack. All we can focus on, for the moment at least, are the current players or those who have played for us at some stage during their careers and gone on to greater things. Not all of them with our blessing, either. We have watched young players whom the club nurtured from nothing kick us in the teeth by refusing to sign new contracts and moving abroad on a free transfer, thanks to the Bosman ruling, so the club gains nothing. Such players aren't popular with the fans, who demand loyalty from their team.

Yet while players who abandon us are one thing, we can at least understand that to a certain extent. Bringing in problems is something else, and we at Watford have suffered with our very own Judas. A player whom no true Watford supporter would ever have signed in their worst nightmare, yet whom the manager signed without realising how some fans would feel. As the Hornets dived headlong into Division Two under Glenn Roeder, we desperately needed a new striker. Paul Wilkinson, who had previously played for Watford before moving to Middlesbrough, came back to the club on loan and really looked the part. Although rumour had it that he was not the most popular man around the dressing-room, he did the business where it mattered, on the pitch. Despite this, Roeder didn't buy him but went for Kerry Dixon, an ex-scummer, instead. Here was a player who was hated by Watford fans because not only had he played for our local rivals, which was bad enough, he had actually scored goals against us in local derbies. Goals that broke our hearts. Yet those in charge happily gave him a contract. To this day, we still can't believe they could have been that stupid. It was the first time we had ever heard a player wearing yellow, black and red booed when he came out to warm up, and we have to admit that the two of us were as loud as anyone. The club was experiencing so many problems at that time that they eventually invited a few supporters in to express their views and suggest areas where they felt the club could do better. For some inexplicable reason, the two of us were invited and the most heated exchange during the whole meeting revolved around the signing of Dixon. One half of the room claimed that the 'true' fans didn't care about his past links with L*t*n, he was a Watford player now. The other half, shall we say, begged to differ.

In the following weeks, tensions ran so high that during the away game at Southend, some Watford fans fought among themselves, resulting in one broken arm and a few severed friendships. We found it difficult to support the side when Dixon played, as we always had the suspicion that he wasn't really trying and was, in effect, still playing for 'them'. We just couldn't trust him and it hurt our pride to see him in a yellow shirt. Some of our regular companions at Vicarage Road even stopped going until he had left. While some will think that pathetic and futile, that was how strong the feelings were. When he left, it was a happy day and, as if to prove a point, his Watford career included not one goal and another relegation. Cheers, then, just another result to the scum.

Of course, we at Watford are not alone and the boardroom dictators within football don't stop at signing unwelcome players. Down in the East End, things have gone from bad to worse at the New Den. Millwall very nearly found themselves going out of existence during the 1996–97 season and are in desperate need of immediate success in order to survive. Even their shares were suspended for a time, being worth the staggering sum of one penny each. In a situation like that, you would think that those in charge would show a bit more awareness of local feelings than to appoint an ex-West Ham player as their new manager. Billy Bonds achieved god-like status at Upton Park and he played a major part in keeping West Ham head-and-shoulders above their rivals from Millwall. What do the board think the reaction will be from the fans? Do they honestly think he will be accepted, trusted? What reaction do they expect if things don't work out, and quickly? Up at Everton, the same mistake was made when they announced they were considering the ex-Liverpool star John Toshack for the position of manager. Toshack has proved himself to be an outstanding manager in Europe and could have been just what Everton needed. Yet the reaction of the fans sent the board a very clear message, and that message was no. Supporters threatened to send season tickets back, requested refunds if his appointment was confirmed and inundated the club with letters and phone calls expressing their anger. It was clear that many supporters would rather suffer than put their faith in 'one of them'.

You see, football isn't rational. In almost every other area of our lives, we want to better ourselves, we want to succeed and will do almost anything in order to get what we want. In football, we must win and nothing must stand in the way of that – except the appointment of anyone that has ever played, managed or worked for 'them' in any way, shape or form. Success must be *ours*, totally ours, and we would rather suffer than have to give any acknowledgement for it to 'them'.

Down here in the basement, we still have the boy next door. It is likely that we will bump into the local hero down the pub or in the chippy, because he lives, drinks and shops with us. He is not isolated or kept at arm's length, and he lives with having the joy of victory or the anger of defeat right in his face. Does that make him try harder? Will he run faster? Tackle quicker? Many would argue not, but we're not so sure. Even the biggest donkey at the club can become a god overnight by scoring the winner in a derby match. He will, as a result, always hold a special place in our hearts. If he just happens to be a local, a supporter himself, then he need never be found wanting for anything ever again until his dying day. Long live the local hero!

On the other hand, if one of your lads gifts a goal to the scum or has a nightmare of a game, then even if it is his only nightmare of the season, it will live forever. Not just in the thoughts of his own fans, but also in the minds of those down the road, as David from Ipswich explains:

## SON OF A GUNN

I wasn't around in the seventies or eighties. I missed the likes of Muhren and Mariner, Mills and Brazil. I wasn't even quite there for the Cup final, way before my time. Like most kids, I watched football on the telly with my dad (not a football man) and kicked the ball around in the park with my mates. It took me a while to realise that there was life aside from Liverpool, Everton, Villa, Arsenal or Spurs. It wasn't until I was finally taken on a trip arranged by my sports teacher that I arrived at Portman Road and became born again. I have been following the club for just six years now.

I have had my favourite players during those years, those that have given me hope at times of despair only to tail off, leaving me with yet another wasted season to look back on. Somehow, I can't bring myself to the hero-worship most people involved with football seem to crave. I hear all the old boys reminiscing about the glory days and find it hard to think that I'll look back on the present crop with the same fondness. At least, I hope not. Surely it must get better one day!

Don't get me wrong, I love the club like nothing else on earth and count the days until the next home fixture, but I have an awful confession to make, one that will have any fan spitting their coffee out in disgust. You see, my favourite ever player plays for 'them', the Budgie-shaggers, No-hope City. I can hardly bring myself to say it, but every now and then a player comes along that lifts you out of your seat. A player that can turn a game in a second with the flick of a hip. His skill in the air, his ball control and his hair are second to none. No one person, male or female, has ever given me such pleasure. When everyone around him is doing their average best, he will stand above all others and hope springs eternal.

All of us have, in our lifetimes, known places and people that, when they re-enter our minds, bring a warm smile to our faces and a glow into our lives. Bryan Gunn, I love you.

This man, the Budgies' goalkeeper, has caused his own defence more problems during the derby games I have seen than all our forwards put together. His ability to completely miss the ball when trying to find Row Z has brought a ray of sunshine into the lives of so many people down here in deepest Suffolk that he should be given the freedom of the county for his services to the community. The man is a star.

Not only has this god among men saved his greatest fuck-ups for the derby games, but they are so good that you never know when they will turn up next on television. With so many programmes centring on sporting cock-ups, I urge the man to apply for membership of Equity, the actors' union, in order to recover what must be some kind of huge royalty payment. Beadle pays £200 a time, so I hear.

All those little Budgies must be falling off their perches after supporting a man for so long, only to be let down so badly. It's amazing to think that after such loyal service to a club going nowhere, it will be the supporters of the team you love to hate that will remember you with the most fondness.

Now, I must nip around the corner and ask our number 9 what the fuck he was playing at last Saturday.

# PART TWO
# Home And Away

_____

# Chapter 3

# It's A Family Affair

If you take football out of the equation, families are the most important thing in most people's lives, and quite rightly, too. That may seem a little trite, but let's be honest, given the choice between being with the wife on a Saturday afternoon and watching your lads, where would you be?

As a football fan, it is inevitable that at some time or another, your love of your club will intrude on the domestic bliss that can hopefully be found as you walk through your front door. Be it the joy of victory or the despair of defeat, the wife, girlfriend, kids, etc, will soon get to know all about it. However, if the game concerned is a derby game, then the nerves will have begun the week before and while victory will bring joy to the world, defeat means a mood bordering on the suicidal. It must be hell living with a footie fan, as both our wives will almost certainly testify.

Still, when things go wrong, other halves have a knack of sticking the knife in where it really hurts, as K. from Birmingham relates:

## THE BITCH FROM HELL

A few years back, I finally got myself separated from the bitch from hell. We had been together for over six years

39

and it had been a complete nightmare. She didn't have any understanding of what football means to a bloke, and like a prat I went along with that for the first few years. I even went two seasons without a season ticket because I knew I would miss too many games due to shopping outings and visiting the out-laws.

The only thing that kept us together for so long was my two boys, Craig, who is now nine years old, and Darren, who is seven and a half. Like every bloke, I prayed for boys so that I could play football down the park with them and take them down St Andrews to cheer on the Blues. Mind you, that was where things started to go wrong because 'the bitch' wouldn't let me take them until they were both over five. She said it was because it would be too rough for them to go, and like a mug I always did what she wanted, anything for an easy life. It was hell having to watch the results staring at the Radio Rentals shop window every Saturday, or diving into the nearest bookies.

Don't get me wrong, she was a great girl when I met her. But as soon as we were married, she put the claws in. When the time to leave eventually came, nothing prepared me for what the vindictive cow was to do, once I had the bottle to leave her.

At first, she was OK with me seeing the kids, but I had them for the day on Sundays, so I couldn't take them to the footy. At least I had the chance to go and watch the lads whenever I wanted, so I managed to live with that. After about a year, she moved in with this lad, a complete doormat. He watches all his football on Sky, comes from Bromsgrove, owns a Liverpool shirt and goes to watch them once a season if he's lucky. In other words, he is a knob.

I really love my kids, they are the most important thing in my life and if anyone did them any harm I would kill them, so you can imagine my horror when I went to pick them up and Darren came running out wearing a Villa top. I went fucking mad and shouted at him so loudly that he burst into tears and ran back into his mum. I ran up the path after him, screaming at the cow to find out what the fuck was going on.

His mum said that he had asked for a Villa shirt after her new man had taken the boys to watch them play Liverpool at Villa Park the week before. It was what Darren wanted that was important, not my wishes. I couldn't believe what I was hearing. He had taken my sons to that shit pit. I wanted to rip his fucking head off, how dare he put my sons in that situation? I could have killed him. Craig was standing there in his Blues shirt, shouting at his mother that she knew I would go mad. I love that boy. The boyfriend is a prick, I know, but she had done this just to get at me and used my own son to wind me up. You can't get much lower than that.

I had to go outside and sit in the car in order to calm down, and told her to send Darren out when he was ready. Craig came out and sat with me straight away, as his mum would have whacked him for shouting at her. He told me he had worn his Birmingham shirt under his coat and cheered Liverpool for the day, which cheered me up no end. What a star. Darren came out after about 20 minutes, minus the shitty shirt. I felt so guilty. All his eyes were puffy and swollen, the poor little sod. It wasn't his fault, he didn't have a clue what he had done. I started the car and drove them straight to St Andrews. We sat in the car eating a bag of chips, as I tried to explain to a seven-year-old how important this place was, and what it meant to his dad for him to love this place as well.

Once he had stopped playing with his Power Ranger, we got the football out of the boot and had a kick-around in the road. It made me feel better and maybe one day, he will realise what an important turning point it will prove to be in his life. Like any father, all I want is the best for my kids and to protect them from evil.

I hate that bitch for what she did to us that day. I've

had a word with the idiot boyfriend and he won't be taking them down there ever again – Craig has promised to ring me if he ever tries. Both boys will be coming to games with me from now on, as I can't risk that happening again. I threatened her with a custody battle if she refused.

And on a similar theme but from a different perspective, Brian from Nottingham has another problem with mums, dads and local rivals:

## COUNTY

Like most young lads, the love affair with my club came about through my older brother and my dad. I can't remember a time when we weren't messing about with a ball, and it was always the same stuff, 'County this' and 'County that'. They were both mental for them, and of course that rubbed off on me.

I was always moaning that they wouldn't take me to games, but when I was about 10, I think, Dad started taking me as well and the three of us would always sit as near to the halfway line as we could get. It was magic. County were a good side back then, and we got to see some great games. As I got a bit older, all the replica-shirt fashion started and of course we all had them and wore them till they were rotten, but that was it back then. Local lads, local side and never any real trouble. I mean, we lived within walking distance of the ground, so most of the time we were at home to catch the results.

Well, when I was 12, my mum and dad split and although he still took us to games for a while, he ended up moving to Ipswich with his job, so he could hardly ever make it. My brother then went and joined the navy and Mum wouldn't let me go on my own, so I was stuck. It was a right bummer, I can tell you. Twelve years old and spending every other Saturday sitting in the garden, listening to the crowd noise. Magic!

Anyway, when I was about 13, my mum met this new bloke. He was all right really, but the thing is that he was a poxy Red, Forest through and through, and used to give me real grief. All I got was, 'County are crap' (as if I didn't know that), 'Forest are superb', blah, blah, blah. He even had one of those stupid little kit things in the back window of his car and an old 'Don't follow me, follow Forest' sticker as well. It used to drive me up the bloody wall. When the two of them started to get a bit closer, he even started to moan at her if I wore my County shirt when we went out together, saying it was embarrassing! Cheeky sod. He even tried to convince her that I shouldn't go to County but that he would take me to see Forest instead! I mean, what could have been worse? Even my mates were starting to believe that I'd turned Red, which was well out of order. But the worst thing was, when I moaned to my dad about it he wasn't really that bothered, because he'd got a new girlfriend as well and he even liked this bloke a bit, despite the fact that he was Forest. My brother was no better – not that I ever saw him anyway, because he was halfway round the bloody world most of the time.

Eventually, the nightmare became a reality and he moved in with us. I tried to put her off the idea, but it was no good. One of my mates even suggested that I told her he'd touched me up, but not even I could do that, although I did think about it for a while. He then started going on about my room and all the pictures on the wall, but in the end even my mum could see he was getting on my tits and he left me alone after that.

Not that I gave a shit, because as soon as I hit 14 she let me go to County on my own – better late than never, I suppose – and the home front settled into a routine of neutrality. No talk about County or Forest allowed, and that was the way it went on until I left home last year. Still, I did give him a bit of shit last season, what with them getting kicked out of the Premier League. I mean, you can't let things like that go, can you?

Of course, as blokes, we are only too aware that while our hatred of local rivals is one thing, the allure of a woman, good or bad, is quite another. However, this can bring problems of its own, as Stevie from Sheffield explains:

## IN-LAWS

When I met my wife, a good few years back now, I had no idea that I was getting myself into something that would bring me a great deal of pain as well as pleasure over the next 15 years. I'm not talking about our marriage, but about the fact that here I was, a Wednesday season-ticket holder, and her folks were mad-keen United fans. Not only that, but her two brothers were, shall we say, 'at it' most Saturdays.

Now as you can imagine, all this came out after we'd been going out a few weeks, and I almost dumped her when it did. I mean, I'd always said that I wouldn't go out with inbreds, but because of her family she always assured me that she hated the game, so I sort of put up with it. After all, we all know that love is blind.

The first time I went home to meet her folks was, to say the least, an experience. She obviously hadn't told them which club I supported and so when they asked, I just said I didn't follow football much and the conversation moved on to other topics. Later on, though, the two twats turned up and obviously took great exception to me being with their sister. The glares across the front room made that quite plain, but the old man was all right and so they just kept grunting in that very attractive way United fans do.

Everything went fine for a few weeks and then one night, the two brothers got me on my own in the kitchen and began grilling me about football. One of them had obviously been asking around, because it was clear that they knew I was a Wednesday fan. In the end, I just owned up – why the fuck not, I'm not ashamed of it – and they went mad. I just stood there and took all their abuse and then told them that not only was I Wednesday, but that the relationship had progressed and it was now at the stage where I was knobbing their sister. Thankfully, the old woman came in at that point and, totally oblivious to what was happening, told me to go into the front room. The twats followed me in there and told the old man that I was a Wednesday fan. He went mad as well and told me to get the fuck out of his house and never come back, which set my bird off and then the mother, and this almighty row develops. In the end, I just stood there listening to it all. It was great, although I would imagine even the old woman would have lost it if they'd told her that I was deflowering her little girl on a regular basis!

After about 10 minutes, my bird grabs me and drags me out – and the two twats followed me, so I thought, 'Here we go . . .' But they just started giving *her* verbal for letting a Wednesday fan shag her! I couldn't take that – she was my bird, after all – so I started to give them verbal back, and one thing led to another and they kicked the shit out of me.

After that, I kept seeing her but avoided going to her house like the plague. On the few occasions I saw her family, her brothers wouldn't speak to me at all and the old man would just about manage a grunt when I walked in the room.

That was years ago now, of course, and we're well married now although the wedding ended up in a ruck, as the two brothers were the only Blades among 50 Wednesday lads. We're at least on speaking terms now, but I have to say, if my daughter ever brings a Blade round my house, there'll be fucking murder!

Women have been the ruin of many a good football fan.

Keeping him away from the ground to do menial, mind-numbing tasks is all part of the female armoury. Some of them have even had babies on a Saturday afternoon, for God's sake! However, while they try these tactics and are renowned for extracting revenge in any number of sadistic fashions, a good strong bloke can usually win through and occasionally have a go back. We hear a lot of stories like that, but recently, we heard a tale from a man who got it all wrong, and in the worst possible fashion. What makes it worse is that he is, like us, a Watford fan and was, in fact, once the person to be found inside the 'Harry the Hornet' costume on match days. Sad though this tale is, nothing could be as sad as that.

## DUMPED BY A SCUMMER!

It was April 1995 and I was on the verge of graduating from the University of Hull with an Honours degree in Law. Three years of pissing up the wall, a bit of studying here and there, watching Watford flirt with relegation and, of course, flirting with any female who would give me the time of day. This was par for the course of my university life. But in my final few weeks, I committed the cardinal sin of pulling – and worst of all, I fell for a scummer.

We had only recently got a point up at Shitworth Road; 1–1, as it turned out, and in fact the game was the only half-decent derby between Watford and the scum for ages. We hadn't beaten them for over ten seasons, and even then only in the Anglo-Italian Cup, but all that was behind me as I looked forward to another season in Division 1, contemplated life after graduation and wondered how I was going to afford beer at £2 a pint! I had no money to my name, but that night I had managed to get pissed in the Union with everyone else, as this was to be the last big piss-up before the final exams, just three weeks away. Inevitably, once the mandatory alcohol intake had been consumed, the singalongs started and as was usual, they soon turned to football.

The good thing about being in a university town of nearly 20,000 students was that there were supporters of every team in the land. Unfortunately, this also meant that while there were plenty of people to have a good old sing with, there existed a few deluded souls who supported Shit Town – and tragically for me, *she* was one of them.

That particular night, I had had my share of stick. This guy James, from Reading, had been waiting for over two years for his lot of sheep-shagging wankers to beat us and it had finally happened a few weeks before: 4–1, a travesty, and he hadn't shut up about it since. Then a couple of scummers had their usual pop about beating us 4–2 back in September and I had had enough. No one should ever be allowed to mention that game again. That was it. I was off, gazing over the seasons' highlights from 1981–84, the glory years. Those were the days. But then I figured no, retribution would be mine. Short of being either astonishingly offensive or physically violent, I had no way of getting the higher ground against filth like scum fans and so my rationale changed. I would make the girl who joined the chants from the sidelines fall in love with me and then I would dump her. I would fight the wankers from within and would break her resolve until the name of Watford Football Club really hurt her!

In that moment, I was transformed from a man depressed into a man possessed. This would be better than violence, it would be a form of torture. I'm no fighter, I prefer to spend my time using my energies singing and chanting against the vermin to stamping on their heads, but now I would finally get to do my bit against L*t*n. So I set about pulling her, which, to be honest, wasn't too difficult. She was obviously impressed by the beer stains and my ability to burp in time to 'Rule Britannia', and the offer of a pizza was enough to secure her entry to the lair they called my bedroom.

The plan was a good one; the execution, however, was not. I had planned to go to watch Berwick Rangers v Greenock Morton in some godforsaken hell-hole the following day with a bunch of similarly sad football freaks from the FSA, but chose instead to spend the day with the woman I hoped to corrupt. However, it soon became clear to me that my plan was fatally flawed, for I had fallen for her in a big way. As a result, I thought the best way out of the mess would be to try and keep football out of the relationship and try for a normal 'boy-girl' thing.

Well, that didn't work either. I tried to pretend that it didn't matter that she was scum, but what made it worse was the fact that, like me, she actually worked for the club on match days. Her tales of her encounters with 'Ginger Scum' Hartson or 'Showaddy-fucking-waddy' Oakes drove me to distraction, while I could only respond with my tales of life as 'Harry the Hornet' and how I got to drink with the players in their bar after games. It was hopeless, each tale driving a stake through the other's heart worse than the one before. From then on, we realised that this wasn't a relationship, it was a competition. I casually introduced her to as many of my Watford-supporting mates as possible (not easy when you're at Hull University), while she decided to invite up a couple of L*t*n likely lads to put the wind up me one weekend. All for her amusement, of course, but neither I nor the two scummers saw the funny side and a quick warning from one of them to 'Watch it with our women, you wanker', as I took a piss one night, convinced me that this was getting a little too hazardous for my liking.

Things went from bad to very bad to irreconcilable in the space of a single day. My close friend Mark, who has supported Watford since the sixties, called me a traitor and suggested I was spawning the devil's child. Then I lost it when her mum wound me up on the phone and I ended up calling her 'scum'! Hardly the best way to treat your potential in-laws.

I was unceremoniously dumped on the spot and was rejected at all turns. She had foiled my original plan of domination and torture and had made me compromise the values to which I had held so dearly. Not only that, but she had spat them all back in my face. I had become a traitor to my kind and was left a man without honour. Now I forever have the shame of sleeping with the enemy, while all she has is that smug feeling of one-upmanship.

I hate her.

When one talks about football, families and local rivals, it is inevitable that talk will, at some point in the conversation, turn to Merseyside. We had a long piece written about the feelings between the Red and Blue halves of Liverpool and then we received the following letter, which says everything far better than we could:

## YOU'LL NEVER WALK ALONE

The whole of the country seems to have this fixed view that all Scousers get on like Siamese Twins and that we all just love to see the other lot do well. Well, I am sorry to shatter the media illusion for you, but that just isn't true. The images portrayed by the ex-pros, comedians and dear old Cilla don't mirror the feelings of a vast number of fans up in this part of the world.

I remember the first time I ever really bonded with my dad, I know the date off by heart: it was 28 October 1978. He wasn't a really big football fan and he hadn't yet taken me to watch a live game, but he would listen to the football on the radio every Saturday while doing stuff around the house. His dad had always been an Evertonian and the effect had brushed off on him. I remember hearing this almighty shout that afternoon and Mum rushing past to see what was going on. I followed, but before I arrived she was on her way back, telling me to take no notice of my father as he was acting up like a small child. I had to look. He called me over to the car and explained that Andy King had just scored for Everton against Liverpool at Goodison. He told me Mum didn't understand, but at the time, neither did I. I had never seen him this excited before. He became more and more excited as the minutes ticked by, and promised that he would take me to see Everton play their next home game if the score stayed the same. So we bonded; come on, Everton, come on. The final whistle went, 1–0 to Everton. It was the first victory over Liverpool in seven years, the first Everton win in my lifetime.

I don't know why, but I went to school that Monday morning and shouted 'Everton!' throughout every play break, finding a few new friends and enemies along the way. Suddenly we weren't all together, and for me it's been the same ever since. Dad didn't take me to the next game, but he did keep his promise soon after and I was hooked. Liverpool went on to win the Championship that year but the shout of '1–0' still seemed relevant to a six-year-old and his comrades. Liverpool went from strength to strength while Everton just sort of existed, and I kept quiet on the cheering front. I always remember feeling as if Everton were looked upon as being like cute little children, getting patted on the head when things almost went right. In 1984, that all changed as Everton made it to two Cup finals. The Milk Cup final defeat against Liverpool that year seemed to just back that feeling up, but following the FA Cup win over Watford (*Thanks to a very dubious goal and a shit referee – Ed/Dougie*) things became very different. With the team starting to finally enjoy some success, Dad seemed much happier to let me go and watch them on my own.

The next season, Everton were at their greatest and in October won at Anfield with one of the greatest goals ever seen. The attitude of the Liverpool fans changed that day, for the first time in 15 years, because they were hit by the realisation that they were no longer the best team on Merseyside and they couldn't handle it. Liverpool won nothing that season; Everton won the Championship, very nearly the domestic double, and capped it off with the European Cup-Winners' Cup. Most of the people of this city had for years cheered on the Reds as they flew the flag for British football in Europe; it was very different during our moments of triumph. For many, their only concern was bringing home the European Cup, putting themselves back on top: 'You see, Everton still haven't won the European Cup, though, have they?' The goodwill was in very short supply from their supporters, who then dragged English football to a new low at Heysel.

The next season couldn't have been worse. Liverpool bounced back to win the Championship, beating us by just two points. All attention focused on the first all-Merseyside FA Cup final; Liverpool won 3–1 and secured their first ever domestic double. I'll never forget the reaction of their supporters. The return of the smug patting of the head will never be forgotten. As far as they were concerned, Everton had had their moment, now it was time to get back in their place.

That made many up here angry and the club came out fighting: 1986–87 and the Championship was ours again, stolen back. It was this period that drove the wedge home for many Scousers, from both sides. The constant yo-yo of the clubs' fortunes led to a desire to be one-up on the enemy that, for many, had never been experienced before, or since.

Everton seem destined to play second fiddle to our neighbours, looking for the derby match as our only source of consolation. Imagine being in that situation, sharing a city with that hanging over you day in, day out. Having it rammed down your throat in the pub, at the shops, at work. Constantly reminded that you're second best in a city of two. If you think we all get on in

a situation like that, then you need your head looking at.
Incidentally, not all of us like the fucking Beatles, either.

It would, of course, be impossible for the two of us, as brothers,
to talk about families and not write something about our own,
because contrary to popular belief, we do have a dad.

### BALLBOY

When the two of us were much, much younger, Boxing
Day would mean a visit to our nan and granddad who,
as it happened, lived not half a mile away from White
Hart Lane. As all fans know, Boxing Day is good for one
thing only and that is football, and so our old man, in his
endless quest towards turning us into Tottenham fans,
would take the opportunity to drag us down to White
Hart Lane.

Back in those days, the Boxing Day fixture was always
the local derby clash and the old man felt that witnessing
a north London derby would finally clinch our support
for the Yids. Dad had been building us up for this day
for weeks and we were all really looking forward to
witnessing what we hoped would be a classic encounter.
Unfortunately, our old fella had overlooked the fact that
about 50,000 others had made the same arrangements,
and on our way to the match, it became clear that we
had no chance of getting in. The game had become a sell-
out well in advance. We did feel sorry for him, because
not only would he miss seeing his beloved Spurs play, he
also had four very pissed-off kids tugging at his coat-
tails and thinking what a prat he was.

Now on the same day, Fulham, who were riding the
crest of a wave at the time, were playing their local derby
with Chelsea at Stamford Bridge, and in all honesty we
would much rather have gone to that match anyway. One
of Eddy's best friends is a lad named Keith and his dad
was Fulham through and through, and had very much

the same idea as our old boy in trying to get his son to carry on the family tradition of following the same club. At that time, they had George Best and Rodney Marsh in the side and he used to take us down to watch them whenever he could. Eddy will happily admit that he enjoyed being taken down to Craven Cottage more than any other ground in those days, despite the fact that the Fulham fans were hardly the most vocal when it came to supporting their team (no change there, really) – half-hearted renditions of 'Fulham . . . Fulham . . .' or 'There's only one Georgie Best' being about their limit. Much more entertaining was Keith's dad's habit of rubbing his hands together in excitement whenever Fulham got a corner or something. He would rub them so fast that you could almost see sparks flying. Perhaps he was a scout master on the quiet. There used to be a group of blokes that stood behind him taking the piss every time it happened, but nobody ever had the heart to tell him. So in our disappointment, Eddy suggested to our dad that we try and make our way down to West One and take that game in instead. The poor sod had no choice. After all, it was Christmas.

We arrived about half an hour before kick-off and the place was rammed. In typical Stamford Bridge fashion at that time, the ground was littered with the usual array of discarded weaponry, but we still thought we were in with a chance of seeing a game. However, just as we were getting near the turnstiles, the police announced that the ground was full and the gates were closing. Bollocks, locked out twice in one day. In all fairness to our dad, he did decide to hang around and try asking everyone and his mate if they had any spare tickets. He even asked all of us kids to look really upset as he went up and pleaded with a copper to let these poor, miserable children in, as their festive season would be ruined if they had to miss the Blues in action. Eddy even got a whack around the head, although to this day he's unsure if it was to get a genuine tearful reaction for the benefit of the said officer, or if it was for calling Dad a prat and telling him that he had ruined our lives. Whatever, it had the desired effect.

It became clear that we were fighting a losing battle and as the crowd dispersed, we had finally decided to make the move ourselves when the most amazing thing happened. Dad had just rounded us up and cleaned Eddy's face up when this bloke came over wearing a Chelsea club blazer. He asked the old man if we were his kids, then explained that one of the ballboys hadn't turned up and they needed a replacement. He then turned to one of our brothers – whom we will not name, for fear of retribution and subsequent hospital treatment – and asked him if he would like the gig. As you can imagine, competition for this position was, shall we say, fierce. Dougie, quite simply, favoured the threatening and violent approach, while Eddy adopted the tactic of willing instant illness, leaving him the opportunity to take over. Our other brother, rather astonishingly, was totally indifferent. Never the world's greatest football fan anyway, being dragged around London on a cold Boxing Day had all but wiped out any lingering interest in the game and it has never returned, despite our best efforts to educate him. The two of us were pleading with this man to take either of us instead, but Dad held us back and our brother was guided away, giving us the wanker sign behind his back as he went. How could the Good Lord be so cruel to children at this time of year?

To add insult to injury, we were dragged back to Tottenham for an afternoon of despair and moaning, begging for sympathy from our mother who repeatedly told us not to be such miserable, selfish little shits and to stop sulking, the distant noise from White Hart Lane providing what surely must be the most ironic background of all time. Our brother arrived back at around 6.30, in the taxi provided by the club. As you can imagine, he was fucking full of it and to make matters worse for us, every moment had been caught by the television cameras. He went on and on about how he had put the ball down for George Best to take a corner, the George Best sent from heaven to entertain *us*, and even though total hatred was still burning inside, we couldn't help but be impressed by that and so it was agreed that he would replay the entire match, and the magic moments, with Eddy's new Subbuteo set once we got home.

Our brother was obviously mad keen to do this from the moment we walked through our front door. Whether he was milking the last drop of jealousy from us or still riding high on the excitement is difficult to say, but it was felt that stuffing him at Subbuteo would at least give him some kind of payback for our suffering. It was at this moment that our mother walked in and asked if he had put some clean underwear on and what he had done with his dirty pants. Now, most people love their mother for many reasons, but it is fair to say that ours became even more endearing for what she was just about to say. The words 'dirty pants', when used about someone else, are always music to a young boy's ears and this was no exception, especially when our brother began desperately to try and shut her up. 'What do you mean, "dirty pants"? Has he crapped himself?' It was only meant as some kind of cheap dig at him, but then the truth came out. 'Didn't he tell you? He wet himself in all the excitement, just as he ran out of the tunnel.'

Our brother was kneeling at one end of the Subbuteo pitch, with Eddy at the other, and it obviously took a short while for the full impact of those words to hit home. During what would remain one of the greatest moments of his life, our brother had lost control of his bladder through sheer nervous energy. Oh, praise the Lord . . . There is a God after all, He who moves in mysterious ways, and He loves us . . . Praise the Lord . . . Eddy roared as our brother ripped the pitch from underneath the little moulded men, sending plastic flying in all directions. He then stormed out past Mum, screaming obscenities at her. Eddy, of course, immediately relayed this earth-shattering tale to the rest of the family, who were quickly reduced to fits of laughter. Not only had he been found out, but everyone was quick to remind him that his embarrassment was going to be shown on television the very next day.

We were glued to the TV that day. Even a few of my mates were brought in to share the experience, as our brother sat hiding behind a cushion, hardly able to open his eyes. Whenever the camera went near him, you could see him kneeling down trying to cover his embarrassment, it was marvellous. If only we'd had a video back then.

In a strange way, we have to feel a little sorry for him now, because his great moment had been stolen from him. Every time the conversation turns to football, we can see him cringeing in the hope that no one brings up the story. If anyone ever mentions the fact that not many people get the chance to line up a corner for George Best, the response that not that many people piss themselves in front of 50,000 screaming football fans and a watching TV audience of millions, either, is never far behind.

Sorry, Bob, we tried to avoid it, but in the end we had no choice. We had to do it.

But to redress the balance, Eddy relates another tale about our long-suffering brother which will bring shame down upon the two of us.

### 'OI! I PAY YOUR WAGES, YOU TART'

When I first started to watch Watford play on a regular basis, the team were playing in the old Third Division and about to be relegated. The league status didn't matter then, as these men were my heroes. I only watched the games, I didn't really understand what points meant back then, nor did I study the league position. All I knew was that we were playing Halifax at the Vic and I wanted to be there. Once promotion and relegation was explained, football took on a whole new meaning. Every game became important and therefore we started to travel to away games. Dougie was away most of the time, serving his country, as he liked to put it, and so I used to go with our brother Bob. He was great. I had no money, as I was still at school, and Bob used to pay for me to go on the coaches with him. He was as much a Hornet as anyone could have been and we followed the club all over the country as they clinched promotion back up out of the Fourth Division. From Torquay on Boxing Day to Scunthorpe for the Championship, it was a fantastic time to follow the club.

We spent the next few weeks waiting for the fixtures to come out, eager to see what new places we had to visit and when. The first match of the season was away at Walsall. Now that may not be much of a draw to you, but we were counting the days as the expectation grew. We travelled up on the club coaches, as always in those days, and it seemed as though every Hornet in the land was making a beeline for the Midlands. The M1 was full of yellow, black and red; lovely.

Walsall's old ground was much more of a stadium than the cardboard box they have now, a proper footy ground. We had the open end and a small covered section along the side, where the singing and the noise were fantastic. Their fans were making a fair old racket as well and the atmosphere was superb. Then disaster struck: the Saddlers scored, then added a second. That wasn't in the script at all, the wankers. Why is football so shit? At this point, the number of Watford fans swelled as we could see all the lads from the special train running over the bridge at the side of the ground, desperate to get in as quick as they could. The train had been delayed for over one and a half hours and they were decidedly pissed off.

Most of the main lads used the specials back then and when they found out the score, word went around that they intended invading the pitch (a favourite Watford tactic, back then) if Walsall scored again – or at half-time, if the score remained the same.

Walsall continued to push their advantage home and were then awarded a dodgy penalty. Andy Rankin, a god among goalkeepers, never had a clue just how important his penalty save proved to be, as it stopped the majority of the lads from trying to get onto the pitch and at the Walsall end. Within minutes, the Hornets had turned the game completely and pulled back level at 2–2. I fucking love football. The second half saw the lads totally take the piss as we went on to win 4–2. The sun was shining and we were having a ball. Coming from 2–0 down, saving a penalty and then winning 4–2, at Walsall, must rank WFC among the best teams in Europe, if not the world. This was surely football heaven. The party went on well after the final whistle and we travelled back down the M6 singing our little hearts out. Then it all turned a bit pear-shaped as the coach joined onto a long traffic jam and started to develop a rather nasty noise, before deciding that it would go no further.

Our spirits couldn't be dampened, despite the fact that we would have to wait for over two hours for a replace-ment coach to come out and get us. We danced around the cars in the traffic jam and tried to ponce lifts off the Watford supporters that slowly passed us. After about an hour, we spotted a coach that was attracting a lot of attention from the cars around it. It was the WFC players' coach, our heroes. All the lads ran to the coach to cheer the lads on and congratulate them on their famous victory. Bob and I ran up in the hope that we would get the chance to speak to some of the players, or even ponce a lift. They didn't want to know. I'll never forget the look on some of their faces. There we all were, blokes and lads that had followed this club all over the country to cheer them on, and they just looked at us like we were scum. Bob was stopped in his tracks and some of the other lads were getting well pissed off at their attitude towards us; after all, we were only having a laugh. That was the first time I ever heard the saying, 'I pay your wages, you know,' and it stuck deep in my mind there and then.

I looked at Bob, who was shouting abuse at them along with five or six others. They couldn't believe that they didn't at least stop and ask us if we were all right and had things sorted out. It wouldn't have taken much. The coach drove off into the distance and we sat down on the roadside, waiting to be rescued. Bob didn't say a word.

The police arrived and decided that the best thing to do would be to try and get us onto other transport, so they flagged other coaches down and Bob and I were put onto a coach with a load of old biddies on their way back from a weekend in Blackpool. In fact, that was a right result and they had loads of lard to feed us up on. As we walked back home from Junction 8 of the M1, Bob went on and on about the attitude of the players towards us, saying that he would never go to watch them again. It had been a long day and I thought he was just tired. He wasn't. Bob hasn't set foot in Vicarage Road since that day.

Now comes the worst confession I can possibly make. At first, I thought it was just a phase he was going through and that he was suffering from football burnout. Then it happened. About two months later, I was sitting at home on a Saturday night when Bob came in and tossed a football programme to me. Ugh, it was a Shit Town programme. 'What the fuck's this?' I asked. Then he pulled out a scarf. It was orange, white and blue, he was coming out. He had turned scummer. At first I thought it was a piss-take, then in walked his mate Andy, a bloke I never trusted due to the fact that he was not only scum but ginger as well, a nightmare combination in anyone's book. All I could do was sit there with my mouth wide open as Bob went off on one about how he hated the Hornets. He couldn't believe that I could continue to support a side that had so little respect for its fans, and many of the words he shouted have stayed with me ever since.

The attitude of the players and officials that day cost them the lifelong support of my brother and I still can't forgive them for that. Since then, I have never been one for hero-worship; players come and go, as do managers, chairmen and directors. Bob changed clubs like the top shelf of a newsagents over the next few years before seeing the light and pledging his life to the mighty Bath City. I know he looks back on that time, like we all do when we look at old photos of ourselves wearing ridiculous clothes, and thinks: 'Why, oh, why did I do it?' But I can't hide the fact that he felt forced into committing the ultimate footballing sin by the behaviour of the team that day.

# Chapter 4
# Work, Rest and Play

Problems with our families are one thing; problems at work quite another. Indeed, one of the drawbacks of being an active football supporter, never mind an active football hooligan, is that your rivalry is all too often carried over into the workplace. As far as local rivals are concerned, work puts us in situations where we can come into contact with people we will be abusing when the two teams meet. On far too many occasions, what starts out as good-natured banter turns into something far more serious, as the following anecdote from Ian, a West Brom supporter from the Black Country, explains:

### SANDBAGGING

A few years ago, I started a new job at a garage in Wolverhampton and as I walked into the workshop on my first day, it was obvious that my worst fears had come true. Everyone in the place was a Wolves fan and here was I, a Baggie to the core, walking into the lions' den. What could I do? I needed the job, but it was my worst nightmare.

At first, I denied any attachment to football whatsoever – which, considering the way we were playing at the time, wasn't too far off the truth. Thankfully, I managed to get

61

away with it for about six months, but it all went wrong on the day that Graham Taylor left Molineux. Some of them were really chuffed and were going mental, while others were far from happy and were going on about how he'd got a raw deal off the board and all that stuff. Now, you know when you say something and, even as you're saying it, you know you shouldn't – well, that happened to me that very afternoon. I was sitting with a few of the lads in the rest room, listening to the news on the radio, and when they mentioned Taylor, for some bizarre reason I still can't explain, I happened to remark that we all thought Taylor and Wolves deserved each other because they were all wankers. All eyes immediately turned to me and then one of them came out with the immortal line, 'What d'you mean . . . "we"?'

From that moment on, I was fucked. I stood up and swore my true faith and was immediately subjected to levels of abuse and ridicule previously unimagined. I had always believed that having a celebrity ponce like Frank Skinner supporting your side was the worst thing that could happen to anyone, but the shit I got off those wankers was far worse. Word of my announcement spread like wildfire and by dinner time, graffiti was appearing on the walls by my workbench, as well as in the toilet. I resolved to stand and fight my corner.

It's amazing the effect admitting your side are shit has on lowlifes like Wolves fans. They just can't get to grips with it. Every time they made a 'witty' remark about the Baggies and how bad they were, or what a state the ground was or what shit the kit was or what twats the fans were, I agreed. In the end, though, this began to wear me down and eventually, because I wasn't biting, they just turned to personal abuse and pretty soon I'd had enough. As I was walking out of work one Friday evening, one of the mouthy twats started again and, without thinking, I just turned and stuck one on him. The effect on the rest of them was instantaneous. It was as if by having a go at one of them, I had as good as given them permission to kick the shit out of me, and so they did.

I resigned on the Monday rather than go back into work and rang the workshop manager and told him exactly why. From what I heard later on, two of the ones who attacked me were sacked and the rest were given written warnings. Funnily enough, the one who I smacked wanted to get me done for assault, but I think the manager made him back down. Maybe I should have hit the wanker harder.

In a similar vein, working can also give you ample opportunity to take the piss out of your hated rivals, but that can often be a very risky business, as first Billy from London and then Keith from Manchester explain:

### WEST HAM

A few months back, I worked in a big insurance office in the City and it was full of football fans from all the London clubs. We used to have a right laugh at work, talking about what had happened the weekend before and where we'd been. All the usual banter you get among blokes at work.

Well, all that changed when this new bloke joined the firm. Raving mad for Chelsea, he was, and it soon became clear that he would not hear a single word against his beloved Stamford Bridge lads. From then on, the atmosphere changed. If we talked about anything, it was 'Chelsea this . . . Chelsea that . . .' and he became a right pain in the arse. I mean, as a Hammer, you don't want all that shit all day, do you? And so I resolved to get rid of this twat. Not just for supporting Chelsea – we had a few of them already – but because he had fucked up our days.

At first, I started slowly: a bit of graffiti in the lavs, the odd note in his 'in' tray when he was out of the office, that sort of stuff. After a couple of days, it was really winding him up and as no one knew it was me, I could milk it for all it was worth. Anyway, after a couple of weeks I started sending anonymous letters down the line to his computer, and that was when he really freaked. Simple stuff like 'Chelsea run from everyone', 'The Shed is dead, fuck the Shed', that sort of thing. In the end, he was like a bloke possessed. Every time he turned on his computer, a message would be waiting for him; you could almost see the wanker twitching as he did it. It was top. He was accusing everyone from the cleaners to the managing director. But with no proof, he was knackered, which, for me, made it all the sweeter.

Then I did a stupid thing, I sent him a message about Matthew Harding. Nothing really bad, just, 'Hello, Paul, it's Matthew here. Next time you go down the Bridge, please tell Ken the will is under my seat in the directors' box.' He went apeshit and stormed out of work in a right hump. Now, I have to say in my defence, I did feel guilty about that, because I'd gone too far with that one and when the others in the office saw it, they were all very unhappy. They all started accusing each other and eventually, with the whole office at it, someone worked out it had to be me.

I put my hands up immediately, there was no point in doing anything else. I tried to defend my actions by saying what a twat this bloke was being and how he had made work a total pain. This held no sway with the Chelsea lads, who were, to say the least, very unhappy with me.

The next day, when I walked into work, he was waiting for me by my desk. Someone had obviously told him that I had been the cause of his unhappiness and now it was clear that he wanted an apology. I held out my hand, said sorry and started to explain why I had been doing what I was doing, when he grabbed my hand, pulled me towards him and butted me full in the face. He then threw me back across my desk, scattering papers and my computer over the floor, and gave me a kick in the stomach for good measure. With that, he walked out and didn't come back.

I deserved what I got, I've no doubt about that, but at least he left, which was, after all, the whole objective. The other lads kept the whole thing quiet so the bosses never found out why he left, which was good of them, and slowly the office has returned to its old ways. Thankfully, the new bloke is a Hammer, like me. Hopefully, I'll have no worries with him.

## CITY BOY

A couple of years ago, I worked in a large office dealing with customer services, so the place was really busy and full of people on the phone. In fact, it was so busy that the only time you could talk to anyone was when you were on a break, so all talk of football with the other lads was out while we were actually at work.

On the desk opposite me was a bloke called Geoff, and although there were a few City supporters in the place, he was the only one who actually went regularly. I think the fact that we couldn't talk much football was a godsend to him, because he hardly ever had to put up with any shit from all of the United fans.

We still used to wind him up, though. Loads of United scarves, mugs, all that kind of stuff, and everyone used to send the City lads United Christmas cards to cheer them up. But Geoff used to really get the hump about it and in the end, he started to be a pain in the arse. So I decided to see how far I could go with him before he lost it.

Well, at work, the managers had the facility to send messages to the VDU screens of all the operators. We could respond to them, but couldn't contact anyone else. But through fair means or foul, I found out where one of the managers kept their password and I was in. At first, I sent messages to the other United lads, plus the odd joke and as they hadn't a clue who it was, it ended up being a laugh. Mind you, if the managers had found out what was happening, I'd have been sacked on the spot and really, I should have stopped – but you know what it's like when you play close to the edge.

Well, then I decided to have a go at matey opposite me. At first, it was simple stuff: how shit City were, what wankers their fans were, all that stuff. I'd only do about two a week, just to keep him boiling, and he really started to get wound up about it. He reported this to the managers, who checked everyone out and then changed the passwords in the hope that it would stop. But of course, it didn't, because I knew where the passwords were. This bloke was going mental and so were the managers.

The more I carried on, the worse he got. He threatened one of the other lads because he thought it was him, and then had a blazing row with his direct boss, who had accused him of being too sensitive. Now, I knew I should have stopped there and then, but when rumours were flying around that Kinkladze was about to leave the club and dump City even more in the shit than they were already, I just had to send one more. The trouble was, as I was writing, I got a call to go to the line manager's desk and like a twat, left the message on my screen. Of course, someone saw it and they were waiting by my desk when I got back. They gave me a right bollocking in front of everyone. I knew I was in deep shit and could probably lose my job because of the security problems I had been causing, but worse still was the fact that matey across the desk had heard everything and he was glaring at me with a look of hatred in his eyes. 'You're a fucking dead man,' were the only words he came out with, while 'In your fucking dreams, you tosser,' was all I could respond with. In truth, I was more scared of him than losing my job.

The next day, I was summoned to the manager's office, given a severe reprimand and left in no doubt that if I did anything else to piss someone off, I would be sacked on the spot. I was also moved away from my desk and placed at the other end of the office opposite an old dear, so work became even more boring. Still, at least matey couldn't threaten me anymore, so by the end of the week, I had all but forgotten it.

On the Friday night, I took my girlfriend to a club in Manchester and as I walked in, who was the first person I saw but Geoff. He immediately clocked me and from the expression on his face, I thought it would be a good idea to go somewhere else. But my girlfriend had already met up with her mates and so I was stuck.

Later on in the evening, I had to go for a slash and as I hadn't seen Geoff for a while, I thought he had already left, so as I entered the toilets, I didn't give him a second thought. As I'm standing there, knob in hand, my head suddenly made a rapid movement forward and smashed into the wall, and I went down on the deck to find myself staring up at the face of Geoff – and he was not happy. 'You little cunt,' he said, and proceeded to kick the shit out of me until someone else came in and dragged him off me. The police were called and he was arrested, but I was taken to hospital with severe concussion and a few broken ribs.

As a result, he ended up doing three months for assault, primarily because he already had a record for violence – something he hadn't declared on his job application and something that, if I had known, would certainly have deterred me from acting like a twat in the first place. Yes, I know it was my own fault, but Christ, it was only a bit of a laugh. And let's be honest, if you're a City fan, you need something to laugh at, don't you?

For most football fans, the actual game itself is only a part of the attraction. Football is not just an event, it's a whole culture and it allows us males to behave in ways that we never normally would. For example, not many blokes would admit to it, but football provides us with the opportunity to openly show affection in a way that we cannot comfortably elsewhere, for whatever reason. After all, when was the last time you gave your best mate a hug, other than when your lads had just pulled off a major result? Similarly, football allows us to vent our frustrations and anger in an atmosphere that almost advocates it. The stadium environment, no matter what the 'new-breeds' say, encourages us to rant and rave and get it all out of our system in a way that we never could anywhere else. It's all spur of the moment, spontaneous and spectacular. Those are the reasons why we love it. It provides us with much more than just 90 minutes of entertainment, it's a whole culture of excitement.

Away from the game, we supporters spend those tragic days between matches talking, living and breathing football. Football, quite simply, demands to be talked about – be it at home, at work, in the pub or, as Billy from Ipswich explains, even in restaurants.

## *NIGHT OUT*

A couple of years ago, I was with this new bird in a local restaurant. I'd been after this girl for ages and had finally persuaded her to come out for a meal. We'd been there about half an hour and we're really getting on, to such an extent that I'm even starting to fancy my chances for later.

At about this point, these four people come and sit at the table next to us. Nothing strange about that, really, just two couples out for a meal. So I get on with the business in hand, which by now was working out the best time to ask this bird back to my house. Suddenly, I catch a snippet of the conversation at the next table and the word I caught was 'City'.

Now, as you do, my attentions become focused on this

table behind me, and fuck me if they aren't all Yellow. Straight away, I'm off my food and all thoughts of 'afters' vanish as I begin to listen intently to the bollocks they're talking at the next table. Just in case they start to slag off my beloved Town, of course. This bloke is going on and on about City's chances for the rest of the season, how they're certain to get promoted, all the usual load of bollocks, when he finally hits the spot. Ipswich come into the conversation and I am now all ears. This twat then starts to go on about how Ipswich have always been the poor relations of the region, how they'll never get into the Premiership, etc, etc. As if that's not bad enough, the other bloke at the table is agreeing with him! Conclusive proof, if any were needed, that all Budgie fans are thick.

By this time, I'm seething and so is the bird I'm with. In her case, not because of the shit these blokes are talking but because I'm so obviously listening to them, it is becoming embarrassing. She starts giving me grief under her breath, like birds do, but I can't hear that, because these two are entering new realms of twattishness. They're now talking about the future for Norwich as if they're fucking Inter Milan.

I couldn't take it anymore and leant over to their table. 'Excuse me,' I said, 'but I couldn't help overhearing your conversation and the complete and utter shite you're speaking.' As the bird I was with stood up and walked out and these four fuckwits stared at me open-mouthed, I went on to remind them of the glorious history of Ipswich Town and the number of times we had beaten them over the years. I even threw in a few things about Robert Chase and Bryan Gunn for good measure. At this point, the waitress, realising that something was going on, came over and asked if everything was all right. 'No, it bloody isn't,' one of the women said. 'This man is being abusive and rude.' She then glared at me and the waitress told me to leave. 'With pleasure,' I said, and walked out feeling excellent.

As I drove off, the loss of a legover was tempered by the feeling of satisfaction that I had ruined the evening of a Yellow bastard and that they would never forget it. After all, I couldn't have sat there listening to them badmouth my lads, could I? What type of fan could do that?

Football is, of course, not just about the professional or even semi-professional game. Many thousands of us take to the local playing fields at the weekends and thrash about in the local hackers' leagues, in the hope either that we will get discovered by some errant scout or simply that we will make it through to lunchtime, when we can get to the pub. Yet within those Sunday leagues there are many rivalries, both local and traditional, and the passion generated by those games can feel every bit as important when you're out there slogging your guts out. Indeed, how many times have you seen or heard about Sunday morning games deteriorating into outright battles? Exactly.

Football at this level also provides some of the best laughs associated with the great game, as well as some of the greatest memories. We have been told hundreds of stories about the amateur game, some violent, some hilarious. What follows is one such account, which is all the more entertaining for the fact that it proves conclusively that Dougie is not only a crap manager, he is also pretty poor as a player. This is his story:

## THE SUNDAY HACKERS

During my time in the Royal Air Force, I was the manager of a squadron team rooted firmly to the bottom of the station Sunday league. The sad thing was, I was also a member of the defence and eventually got to the point where I dropped myself for our fixture against the side who were top of the table. Tragically, this team also happened to be our greatest rivals, not only on the football pitch but in every sphere of air force life.

Competition and rivalry between our two squadrons

ranged from drinking bouts – and the odd fight – in the bar to bombing runs on exercises. This rivalry was encouraged at every turn by our officers, who knew the importance of 'healthy' competition.

For the footie team, the importance of the fixture was made quite plain in the week prior to the match. Various officers called into our office and made it clear what was expected, while the other ranks merely threatened retribution should we lose. This simply added to the pressure on both the team and yours truly, which was the last thing we needed.

On match day, we all turned up as normal but due to circumstances beyond their control, the other team only had 10 players arrive and no spectators other than a few wives, girlfriends and the odd child. However, as they were superior to us in every aspect of their play, they were quite happy to play us with 10 men, which, if nothing else, was pretty demeaning for our lot. Of course, the inevitable happened and their keeper got seriously hurt in our only attack of the first half and had to leave the pitch. I then offered to go in goal for them, promising faithfully that I would be totally impartial!

Following various warnings from their captain, and bearing in mind that we had only threatened their goal once in the first half, they reluctantly accepted my offer and I took my place in goal against my own team! Such was the lack of skill exhibited by my own side (this gets confusing) that I had nothing to do, but they (the team I was in goal for) still could not score and it looked as though we (my real side) might well get a point. Suddenly, a hopeful punt from our defence released our centre-forward, who came charging towards me followed by their defence, who had little faith in my saving their skin. As he entered the box with me rooted to the line, they hacked him to the ground and the ref awarded a penalty. This meant that I was now stood on the goal-line facing a penalty from my own side, who could well end up securing their (our) first win of the season, against the top-of-the-table side and our fiercest rivals, if it went in. Their (their) whole side were now giving me dire warnings of what would happen if I didn't at least make an effort to save it, while my lot were shouting at me to let it in. Meantime, I was trying to let our centre-forward know that I would go to my left, by using exaggerated eye movements, etc, and it seemed by his wry smile that he had got the message. As he ran up, I dived to my left and he, thinking that I had been telling him to put it to that side, put his shot exactly where I ended up, with the result that the ball hit me and bounced back into open play.

Such was the shock of my actually saving a penalty taken by my own side that their defenders won the ball, screamed upfield and scored while my own team were rooted to the spot in total shock.

Everyone was going mental and I, of course, got the blame for it all. Never mind the fact that I hadn't started the game, they only had 10 men and I had told our centre-forward where I was going to dive. On the Monday morning, I resigned my post and suffered a day of torment at the hands of both my colleagues and the rival squadron, who insisted on telephoning me at every opportunity to thank me for the two points. It was a nightmare.

One thing that may surprise many of you is the fact that while Dougie is to religion what Graham Kelly is to charisma, Eddy is a committed Christian. Many will scoff at that due to the type of books that we write, but each to his own and as Eddy is only too fond of saying, 'It's what the Lord thinks that is important.' However, Eddy's religious inclinations came late in life and his faith has not always been rock solid. What follows is an example of one such test:

## COME JUDGEMENT DAY

I first found my faith at the ripe old age of 27, a good few years after I finished fighting at football and had finally calmed down a bit. Dougie and I were never forcefed religion at home. Dad believed in Elvis and the power of TV, while Mum put her faith in Saturday morning pictures, baths on Sundays and eating your greens.

It was a long and winding path that finally led me to the church situated not 100 yards from my front door, but I got there in the end and soon became a regular at the Sunday morning gig. Peter, the vicar, is a lovely bloke – well, he should be, being a vicar – and he helped me no end in finding my feet as I asked the same old questions he must have heard a thousand times before. Most of the other punters are getting on a bit and you can almost guarantee that the Christmas card list will get a little shorter every year. I think Peter was prepared to put in the time in order to pull in some younger blood.

One morning, I was sitting in the congregation and as usual I wasn't paying that much attention to the sermon being preached. In fact, I was more than likely thinking about yesterday's game, or the club's league position, when I heard Peter mention the name of Saint Graham Taylor. Ah! I thought, some relevance to my own thoughts. I sat up eager to pay attention, as this particular piece was obviously meant for me and me alone. The vicar mentioned the fact that when Saint Graham lived in the parish, he would often attend this church in order to gain some divine inspiration, probably about team selection or something. I couldn't believe my ears. Not only was the Lord himself present in this building, but Graham Taylor had visited as well. For all I knew, he might even have sat on this very pew.

Peter went on to talk about the great man (Graham, I mean) and started to talk about the 'problems' it posed him. I sat confused. Then after 12 months, I found out the awful truth as Peter announced that he was a season-ticket holder at L*t*n and wasn't that keen to see the Hornets do well. To this day, it is the only time that I have ever shouted out in church. I don't know what came over me, but the cry of 'No!' couldn't be held back. Peter looked up and the congregation looked around. My girlfriend grabbed my hand in a 'Shut the fuck up' kind of way, but I turned to her in disbelief, saying, 'No, the vic's a scummer.' A sharp kick in the shin brought me back to reality. I sat for the next hour in total shock. How could I attend a church led by one of 'them'? Was God putting before me the ultimate test? Surely I wasn't ready for this yet, I'd only been at it a year.

As the rest of the congregation went off for coffee, I took time out to have a private chat with the Big Man upstairs. Every one of us has a cross to bear and I soon realised that the vicar had been saddled with supporting a crap football team. Then it struck me. As much as we have a cross, we also have a purpose. After years of wondering why I was here and what it was all about, I had been given *my* purpose. I had been sent to save the vicar.

To this day, the poor man remains unconverted and seems unable to listen to reason. I find it hard to accept that a loving God could make him, a man that obviously has total faith, endure such suffering. To that question Peter has no answer, he just laughs a spine-chilling, devilish cackle. The Lord truly does move in very mysterious ways.

Some of the funniest stories we get told come from the members of our old chums, the police. For obvious reasons, we can never print any details that might incriminate them, like the teams involved or the particular match, because football fans are a vindictive lot.

It may come as a bit of a surprise to you that there are some policemen and women out there that actually like football; it certainly did to us. It's just other fans that they treat like shit. Being a copper at football puts them in a unique position, one that sometimes even makes you a little bit envious. Not only do they get in for nothing but they get the best view, free tea and biscuits and the opportunity to get away with murder. The last of these benefits being particularly welcome when they have to police the supporters of the team they hate most of all, as one people-friendly plod explains:

## 'YOU'RE NICKED, MY SON'

For many years, I used to police the matches at Burnden Park, the old home of Bolton Wanderers. We moved up here from the Home Counties many years ago so that the wife could be closer to her family, and getting a transfer wasn't much of a problem. Being from down south, it was felt best that I policed the away end because the locals, once they had picked up on the accent, would give me shit, especially if they were playing a southern team. That was fair by me, as it made my job easier and the away fans were usually better behaved anyway.

Before I joined the force, I was into football big-time and when I was even younger still, my dad and I were season-ticket holders at our local club. I hate the scum from down the road, so the chance to annoy their shitty bunch of sad gits had me looking forward to this particular fixture for weeks.

Now, at Bolton we used to keep a section of open terrace clear between the home animals and the away fans. During the match, the two lots would usually wind each other up by shouting, but the locals also used the opportunity to spot any faces for outside after the match. It wasn't long after the first lot of away fans arrived that I had a result. They had brought a special up with them and we had been radioed that they had a small mouthy element that looked like trouble. On entering the ground, they made their way straight to the fence and started giving loads of mouth to the locals. It's the same every week, but every bunch of hard men think they are the first. Our usual trick is to move in, push a few around without nicking anyone and stop them leaning on the fence. It shows we mean business and cheers the locals up a little as well.

Well, after what was no more than two minutes, this idiot walks over to the fence and leans on it. One of my colleagues standing on the empty terrace gives me the nod to move down, then grabs this bloke's arm through the railing, bends it back and holds him there. The guy was screaming his head off as I got there. All his mates were trying to explain that he had just arrived and didn't know he shouldn't stand there, as if I gave a toss. He was nicked. I had the cuffs on the free hand, so my colleague let go of the other. As I went to grab it, the lad pulled away and I ripped the arm right off his jacket. For a split second, everything stopped and we just looked at each other. Then he called me an 'effing c**t', which didn't go down that well so I dragged him out. He was obviously a little unhappy and shouting out to anyone that would listen for them to take my number. His mates were going mental at the police we left behind.

I took him around the pitch and into the police room under the main stand, then handed him over before having a quiet word with the sergeant about ripping the coat. He decided the best thing to do was to take his name, put the shits up him then just throw him out. As we were taking down his name and address, he kept leaning over to look at what was being written in the book. The sergeant asked him what he was doing and he told him he wanted my number so that he could put a complaint in. The sarge stood up, grabbed his collar and told him that if he wanted, he would throw him in the cells until Monday and have him up for threatening behaviour, resisting arrest, criminal damage and actual bodily harm. This lad shit it totally. They quickly came to an agreement where he would let him go as long as he didn't see the lad within a mile of the ground for the rest of the day. I was then told to escort him to the exit.

We have a door by the main entrance where we usually throw these lads out, but I had another idea. With the help of a colleague, we took him out and walked him around to where the main bulk of the home fans enter the ground. There are some really nasty lads up here, it's certainly not a good place to be an away fan. We took him up to one of the queues and announced that this young southerner thought he was a bit of a hard man. Then we let him go. I love seeing people who are obviously shitting themselves, trying to put on a brave face. I haven't got a clue what happened to him, if anything, because we went back into the ground. But if he got out of that without getting at least one slap, then I would be amazed. I certainly didn't see him again that day.

Of course, if you have a uniform to hide behind, then you don't even have to be at the match to indulge in a little power kick.

### TRAFFIC PLOD

I've been a traffic cop for over five years now and although I wouldn't swap it for any other occupation, there are times when it can become a little boring, bombing up and down the same stretch of motorway or local high road. The guy I work with is well into his football, just as I am, and on days when it's a bit quiet we indulge in a little game we have called 'Tosser Spotting'.

'Tosser Spotting' involves keeping our eyes open for any vehicle displaying a sticker or scarf of our most hated football teams. Living in north London means there is only one team to support, so anything that is white and blue with a sick parrot on it shines out like a beacon to me. My partner is one of those sad southern gits who follows Liverpool, for some reason, and like most sane people he has an inbred dislike for Man United. We often get to work on match days, which makes the game so much easier as we can pull anyone on the way to the game and hold them for as long as we like. It's lovely to see people sweating, thinking that they will miss the kick-off. You can see that, inside, they want to punch our heads in, but they are desperately trying to hold it together. If you get a car-load of lads, there is usually one that will say something. Once that starts, you have them by the balls because you can play them off against each other: 'The sooner we get this sorted, the sooner you'll be on your way.' I love saying that. You can get them to do anything, take all the gear out of the boot, check the jack works, it's great. Don't think we don't know what you say about us when we let you go. Just remember, we're laughing our heads off at you.

Every Saturday night when I am on duty, I must pick up at least one scum fan. If we have won and they have lost, I'll just take the piss a bit. But if it's the other way around, I'll give the car the full once-over and do all I can to find something wrong. One little trick is to ask them if they go to the games at all, sort of suggesting that I follow 'them' as well. It's great, because they get all hopeful that you'll be lenient with them. Then, when I give them an idea that I follow the Gooners instead and therefore hate Spurs, you should see their faces drop. The best one to do is if you can get fans as they start their journey to an away match, because this will put them behind for the rest of the day and really piss them off.

In the past, I've even got people to remove all the stickers and window-hangers by telling them that they obscure the view and are therefore unlawful. I've told them there is a local gang of kids targeting cars with Spurs stickers on them and breaking their windows, all sorts; people will believe anything a copper tells them, just in case they get nicked. It's not all nasty, though. I'll never pull over a Gooner unless he or she is being totally out of order, and then I'll usually just give them a warning or tell them to slow down. It's exactly the same with my partner and the United fans.

Let's be honest here. Put yourself in my position and you would do exactly the same. Most of the time we're chasing up the motorway, risking our necks chasing car thieves and joyriders. It's exciting, but also a bit hairy at times. If in your job you had the chance for a little light relief, you'd take it – and I am sure there are a few other coppers around the country playing the same little game.

# PART THREE
## Revenge!

---

# Chapter 5
# A Dish Best Served Cold

---

Someone once said that revenge is a dish best served cold, and they were right. Think about it, what's the point of putting one over on someone when they're expecting it? They'll have their response mapped out and, worse, they will know why you're doing it. That's no good. Revenge must be planned, powerful and humiliating but above all, it must be satisfying. Oh yes, revenge is about that smug feeling of self-satisfaction, about knowing that you've got one over on someone who has done you down. Let's be honest, it feels tremendous.

Of course, it's pathetic and childish and if we were all decent human beings, we would laugh such things off and forget them in an instant. But we don't, because human nature isn't like that, no matter who you are or what you do. If you have a rival at work who steals credit for your efforts, you shaft him when you can, just as he will shaft you if you gain the upper hand. It happens everywhere, from Buckingham Palace to the local nursery school playground.

For football fans, of course, revenge takes many forms. For the team, it means only one thing: winning the next encounter. There is nothing else they can do. But for the fans, it means outsinging and it means one-upmanship. That swagger down the street so beloved of us all after our lads have dealt out a hammering to those sad bastards who support the scum from up the road, or round the corner, is all about revenge. A bit of payback for all the defeats and the abuse they give us. It makes us feel superior, better and more important than they are, and it gives us that warm glow of satisfaction.

For the hooligans, revenge means violence. Violence to pay back last year's attack, the ambush the season before last, or even something that happened years ago. Revenge is an integral part of the hooliganism culture and, along with reputation, is what drives it along. Taking 50 blokes to your rival mob's favourite pub, and totalling both it and everyone inside it, is an act of violence calculated to extract revenge, but also to *invite* revenge. It as good as says, 'Come to our place next time and see if you can do better.' The local derby adds to the revenge element that territorial and tribal aspect so beloved of the academics who study us football fans as if we were ants in a laboratory. It's what makes the violence at local derbies more intense than at any other type of game.

There is, of course, another type of revenge. The type which only the individual concerned knows about. Those little acts of malice designed to provide a little light relief from the humdrum existence of everyday life. It may be something very simple. For example, if you have the misfortune to work in a place full of supporters of your local rivals, a poster of *your* lads will do wonders for your morale and have the effect of winding them up – and believe us, it does. Even better, if you can, is to have a screensaver on your computer. This can not only be in your lads' colours, it can also be edited on a daily basis to give up-to-the-minute abuse. And if you use a password, no one can do anything about it! An absolutely top invention.

Sometimes, though, revenge of a more calculated nature is called for. This calls for inventiveness and ingenuity of the highest kind, the kind shown here by David from London.

## BARNET

I'm not proud of this, but a few years ago I actually got a bloke the sack just because he was a Barnet fan. I was working for a company in the City and ended up working alongside this chap who was a season-ticket holder at Underhill. He used to go on and on about what a great little club they were and how everyone knew everyone else and all that stuff, until he really started to get on my nerves. He knew I was a Spurs supporter, but that didn't stop him and he went on and on every time football was mentioned. He drove me up the bloody wall.

Eventually, he started on about my beloved Spurs and how we were suffering with Alan Sugar, how all the supporters were being shafted, etc, etc. Totally true, but not what you want to hear from some half-wit, day in and day out. So after about two months, I could take no more and told him to leave it alone. This just made him worse. Here he was, the supporter of a club only just managing to hang on to League status, giving it the biggie to a fan from a Premier League giant. By moaning about it, I'd made his day. When he told me not to be so touchy, I ruled murder out, decided not to quit and so resolved to take the only option open to me. I had to get rid of him.

It will be difficult to explain how I did it without giving my position away, but suffice to say that as salesmen, we survived on the deals we did and from then on, the contracts that he arranged were, shall we say, hardly the most profitable for the company. Deals were lost because the contracts were sent to the wrong address, or never even sent, and figures were altered without his knowledge. He was dragged up to explain what was happening but couldn't, and eventually, when one deal he set up – subsequently altered by me – lost the company in the region of £10,000, he was hauled up before the boss and fired on the spot.

I almost felt sorry for him as he came out of the boss's office, but remembering the grief he had put me through and the knowledge that I wouldn't have to suffer anymore soon put that feeling to one side. As it happens, I was given the job of dealing with all his fuck-ups, which, as I knew exactly what had happened, not only made me look really good but also earned me loads of commission.

It's an ill wind, ain't it?

Pete from Manchester has suffered enough over the years through watching his football at Maine Road, but he, too, extracted revenge in a very inventive manner.

## EVERY DOG HAS HIS DAY

Unless you live in Manchester, you can't imagine what it's been like being a City fan for the past few years. It breaks my heart to see the amount of silver they've taken into Old Trafford, never mind the amount of money being spent, while we've just struggled from one disaster to the next. And then, of course, there's the piss-taking. All the Red bastards giving us earache about how we're letting the city down and how pathetic we are. It's heartbreaking.

Where I work, there are only about five lads who support City. The rest are all United and it's a nightmare. There's even been the odd fight at work when things get heated, but I'm not into that sort of thing – I'm too old and it's bloody pointless. This has been going on for years and you never get used to it, it's like a great weight on your shoulders that you just can't shake off.

Well, a few seasons ago, United had made it through to the final of the European Cup-Winners' Cup against Barcelona in Holland and four of the Reds at work had decided to take a couple of days off and go out there. As it happens, the four were the worst of the bunch at that time and one of them, in particular, made every day at work a complete and utter misery. And so, a plan hatched in my mind to extract a little revenge.

To save money, they had decided to drive down and as I'd been to Europe many times on holiday, they asked my advice on what driving was like across the Channel and what to take in the car. I told them all the dos and don'ts and also to take a first-aid kit, spare bulbs, etc, etc, but above all, a metal petrol can. Now, as I had one, I told them they could borrow it but due to the rules on the ferry, they had to fill it when they got across the Channel and I had to have it back when they returned.

Well, off they went on the Monday night for the game in Holland on the Wednesday and as they left, a feeling of smug happiness swept over me. You see, inside the petrol can I had lent them was half a tin of syrup, which, for those that do not know, is almost pure sugar. When sugar enters a car engine, it wrecks it within seconds, pure and simple, and that was going to happen to these four bastards as soon as they put petrol in that can and poured it into their fuel tank.

As the week wore on, the feeling of happiness was replaced with one of concern. What if the car seized in the fast lane of a motorway? What if they had no recovery insurance? No one else knew what I had done and I suffered alone.

On the Friday, to my utter amazement, they returned, their trip a total success. United, as if I didn't already know, had won the Cup-Winners' Cup. This, of course, led to new levels of abuse from the four travellers, who heaped even more shit down on us poor downtrodden City fans. I had initially felt relieved when they returned because nothing had happened to them, but now I felt regret. The driver of the car had left my petrol can in the back of the car at his house. Promising to bring it in on Monday, he left along with the others, singing more songs about how great United were.

Strangely, on the Monday, things were subdued in the Red half of the workshop and the reason soon became apparent. As it happened, the four travellers had enlisted another Red bastard to go with them to watch United play away on the Saturday, and lo and behold, they had run out of petrol. Thankfully, it had happened on the way to the game and the syrup-laden sugar in the fuel can had done exactly what I hoped it would. The five of them spent a long and lonely afternoon by the side of a motorway listening to their team on the radio, while the engine, terminally wrecked, sat useless in the front of their car. Of course, I initially got the blame; but they were all too stupid to work out how I could have done it and in the end, they forgot about it.

So in the end, I did get a kind of revenge – but the trouble is, I just can't tell anyone.

As Dougie never tires of telling anyone who will listen, he spent a long time in the Royal Air Force. Over the years, this brought him into contact with people from all over Britain and while this was by no means always a pleasant experience – after all, who, given any kind of choice, would want to spend a couple of months living in a barrack room with a Scouser? – it did bring him into contact with supporters of almost every club in the land.

When you're in this kind of situation, football becomes a common link, a conversational tool to break down barriers and, hopefully, forge friendships which can become lifelong. However, when fans of local rivals are posted together, things do not always run smoothly. What follows are a few examples that came out of Dougie's time in the RAF, the first of which is his own.

## THE FALKLANDS

In 1993, I suffered the unimaginable horror of being posted to serve a four-month tour of the Falklands. This is a time of unspeakable boredom punctuated only by work, excessive bouts of drinking and, depending on which Army regiment is there at the time, fighting.

As someone who stopped drinking some years ago (not because of any alcohol-related problem, but because I am crap at it), who avoids any kind of work with a passion and who would now rather have a decent cup of tea than become involved in any kind of violence, the four months stretching before me as I walked off the plane seemed like an eternity.

Holed-up in a single room, living with loads of blokes in a permanent state of either drunkenness or hangover, I took a decision the like of which I never thought would be forced upon me. I decided to get fit.

Now one thing I do have to say about the Forces is that they like their people to be fit and able, and as I fitted neither of those descriptions, the superb facilities available on the Falklands were soon being put to good use by yours truly. Within a few weeks, I had lost weight and was 'pumping iron' and circuit training with the best of them. Something else happened as well, which was a bit scary: I even started to enjoy it.

It was at this point that I met a bloke called Paul. He was, like me, a reluctant regular in the gym and, like me, looked as out of place as a copy of *Escort* in a dentist's waiting-room. But he was a decent bloke, like me in the RAF and married and, also like me, from Hertfordshire. Stevenage, in fact. We decided to work on our fitness together and eventually got to the point where we would partner each other in any of the weekly competitions. Anything from badminton to basketball. We were both doing well, weight was falling off and everything, but because we were different ranks, we never saw each other outside of the gym.

This was to change one weekend, when I managed to get hold of a daily paper (like gold dust back then) and decided to go to the Christian reading rooms for a coffee while digesting the news from back home. As it happened, Paul was there and we started chatting about families and back home, as you always do in those situations.

Now, for some reason, we had never got round to talking about football. I have absolutely no idea why not, but when we did, the truth came out. For some reason, I had expected Paul to be a Spurs fan, but no, he calmly announced to me, as if it were normal, that not only was he a L*t*n T*wn fan, he was in fact a season-ticket holder down at the allotment. 'You are fucking joking? You're not telling me that you're a scummer?' I asked. 'What do you mean, "scummer"?' he said. 'You're not fucking Watford?' The full horror of the fact that I had been fraternising for weeks with one of the enemy hit home like a Frank Bruno right-hander. In truth, it was clear that he felt the same way, his face a picture of shock and disgust.

There was only one thing to do. Holding onto what dignity I had left, I got up, grabbed my paper and walked off. We never spoke again.

During the same tour of the Falkland Islands, it struck Dougie that many football supporters feel the same as we do when it comes to their local rivals. To set the scene, everyone serving in that godforsaken place does a four-month tour of duty, leaving their families at home. For those below the rank of sergeant, that means moving back into a room shared by three other individuals, which, as you can imagine, is hardly the most pleasant experience in the world. Such is the lack of living accommodation on the island that when your replacement arrives at the end of your four months, he not only takes your job, he takes over your room or your bed. That means you leave on the plane he arrives on and when that plane lands, it is usually the signal for a piss-up. After all, you're going home.

The following anecdote came to light during such a piss-up. The names of the individuals concerned are known, and

## A GEORDIE HELL

It was bad enough having to come to the Falklands in the first place, but finding out that I'd have to share my space with two Newcastle fans was the fucking end. There I was, almost suicidal, with the noise of the plane still ringing in my ears and my predecessor jigging around like a maniac, and I walk in and half the room is black and white. It couldn't have got any worse.

I expected loads of piss-taking but I thought that after a couple of days, what with us all being from the north east, it would start to tail off and we could all start on the other bloke, who was a football-hating Yorkshireman. No fucking chance, they got worse. It was just loads of stupid things: I hung my scarf above my bed and every time I left the room they'd turn it upside down, or I'd get the paper and they'd black out all the Sunderland stuff. It sounds pathetic but I tell you what, it drives you mental after a while. Not only that, but it'd be 'Newcastle this, Keegan that, Andy fucking Cole the other.' It drove me up the wall and in the end, I'd had enough. These two blokes had arrived together and had less than two months left, so I decided to extract revenge. Not just for myself, but for all the Roker lads everywhere.

It was stupid stuff at first, dropping dog-ends in their cans while they were in the toilet or loosening off the tops of the salt pots, things like that. Just enough to provide that smug satisfaction of knowing I'd got one over on them. Not only that, but I wrote everything down so that I could tell them on their last night. After a couple of days, though, I got bored with that and so I started on other stuff. For example, one weekend I knew they were going out on one of the battlefield tours, which meant that they'd be walking all day. Due to the early start, they packed their bags the night before and in the morning, when they were in the bog, I loosened off the top of their drinking bottles, just a tiny amount. Over the morning, though, all their gear and their lunch got damp and they lost their drink. Another time, I dropped a pair of brand-new red underpants in with their washing, with obvious results. Particularly satisfying, as it happened, because a Newcastle shirt was in with the load. Pathetic, really, but it cheered me up no end.

However, while I was enjoying all of this, these two twats were too stupid to realise what was going on and their constant abuse continued. So I decided to step things up a gear. The first stage was the old piss-in-a-can trick. Having emptied my bladder into an empty beer can, I would leave it near their table when we were out and invariably one of them would pick it up and have a swig. Urine actually figured quite heavily in my plans and strangely found its way into bottles of after-shave, cans of coke and the odd half-drunk bottle of wine. A letter home produced a package containing enough laxative to disable the entire island, and my two Geordie room-mates soon found themselves with regular cases of the shits. Not together, you understand – that might have aroused suspicion – but regularly enough to fuck up their social life for a while. I mean, would you go out if there was any danger of your arse exploding?

With their departure almost upon us, I decided that the time had come for the final push. I am almost ashamed to say it, but by now, I was enjoying this sadistic role and devising new forms of attack was getting to be exciting. One of the best I came up with was when one of the two grazed his hand and was given a tube of Savlon to rub into it, three times a day. One night, with the dubious use of a matchstick, I managed to scoop out the Savlon from the top of the tube and replaced it with Deep Heat. By fuck, did he scream!

When the time came for them to leave, I became quite

sad. They knew nothing of my revenge upon them and I had decided that after all I had done, telling them would not be the safest thing to do. They would probably have beaten me to death. But it had helped pass the time for me and I couldn't just put up with abuse from two Newcastle fans, could I? Of course, I couldn't let them go without having a final pop at them and so while they were packing, I managed to slip into their cases a few magazines of the seriously hard-core porn variety. I'm talking animals, S&M, that sort of stuff. When they got back to England, the customs boys did exactly what I hoped they would and went through their cases. From what I heard, the two of them were given a right bollocking and reported to the RAF police. What a result.

And in the same vein, an unnamed soldier writes:

## ONE UP FOR THE BOYS IN GREEN!

About four years ago, for reasons too complicated to go into, I was detailed to do a four-week stint in the guard-room. This was quite a cushy number and I soon settled into the daily routine of issuing passes and keys, all the normal stuff. After the first week, the corporal in charge went on leave and when I found out who his replacement was, I knew that the next three weeks would be a nightmare.

As a Celtic fan, there is no doubt that being stuck in a situation involving close contact with a Rangers supporter is one of the worst things that can happen. The guy in question was one of those types who live in their football shirts and he was rabid Rangers. As soon as he came in, the conversation turned to football and as soon as he knew of my love for all things green-and-white, he started: Championships, Gascoigne, McCoist. All day, every day. It was driving me mental but I managed to keep from losing my rag, as he was, after all, in charge.

And in the Army, it pays to keep your cool.

After the first week, I'd had it. On the previous Saturday, Celtic had lost again and, of course, the Blue bastards had won. Off he went about how great Rangers were and what a disgrace Celtic were to Scottish football. The Pope was a ponce and all Catholics should be drowned at birth; on and on and on. And then I lost it and told him to give it a fucking rest.

As a junior soldier, speaking to an NCO in that manner, particularly one who already hates you, is not the cleverest thing to do and from then on, my daily pattern changed. The guardroom was visited by a cleaner every-day, but I was given the job of cleaning up before she came. All weapon-cleaning, which is a seriously boring job when you have 20 rifles and 10 pistols to do every day, was done by me and me alone, and I was also the resident tea-boy. Complain? Who to? I decided revenge was the only option.

Initially, his hourly cup of tea came in for my undivided attention. The addition of the odd mouthful of phlegm or particularly crunchy bogey being a very effective method of obtaining satisfaction. This soon progressed to such delights as wiping my arse with the tea bag I used for his cup, and even, on one occasion, wiping my knob around the rim of his favourite Rangers mug. My personal favourite, however, involved a cockroach, caught with the ingenious use of some sellotape placed on the floor, sticky side up. As the drink cooled, my little crunchy mate went for a short swim before being rescued at the last possible moment.

From these simple yet humorous beginnings, I progressed to the delights of laxative, that old Forces favourite. I resisted the urge to just dump loads of it into the hot water urn, but gradually increased the dose until his trips to the lavvy seemed to blend into one long dump. That feeling of self-satisfaction was awesome and I lived life in that guardroom with a permanent grin.

My last week was shaping up to be the most nerve-racking because on the Sunday, the Old Firm derby was due to take place at Ibrox. Tragically, my lads rolled over once again and that Monday morning was the worst of all. The cunt sang songs non-stop and took the piss out of me all day. Despite my best efforts with the laxative, he remained cheery beyond belief and I decided that as Tuesday was to be my last day, I would leave him in a blaze of glory.

Every day, this Blue bastard would bring in a Tupperware lunchbox filled with pasta salad. It had already been the recipient of both gob and pubic hair, but now was to be the *pièce de resistance*. When he left the guardroom to do whatever it was he went to do, I took his lunch into the toilet and wanked into his dinner, disguising the 'evidence' by stirring it into this already disgusting-looking mess. His lunch was soon back in the fridge and he was none the wiser. For once, I decided to stay in the guardroom and miss my own dinner, as strangely, I wasn't that hungry. But the in-house arsehole munched on his pasta with a passion while I watched, fascinated. It's a strange feeling watching a bloke eat the fruits of your loins and I was desperate to tell him what I had done, but he obviously enjoyed it, so who was I to spoil that?

My stint in the guardroom finished that evening and he sent me on my way with more abuse and a warning that Rangers would go on and on, winning all before them. I still see him around the unit and he still gives me shit, but as he talks, I still think of him munching away and a wry smile spreads across my lips. One day I'll tell him.

While to many of you that last story will seem disgusting – and we certainly don't recommend it – such anecdotes, particularly from members of Her Majesty's Armed Forces, are far from unique. Over the years, we have heard of people obtaining 'revenge' through many such dubious acts; mostly on the day that they left work, but not all. These have included even more bizarre, yet ingenious, methods, such as the Port Vale supporter who shat in the water tank of the office block he had just resigned from, because his boss was a Stoke fan; the Cambridge United supporter who, on being sacked, placed a dead fish in the back of an air-conditioning unit directly linked to the office of three lads who all watched Peterborough; the Millwall supporter who spent weeks dropping hints to his openly homosexual boss that the new bloke, who just happened to be a West Ham fan, was also gay, with the result that the 'Iron' ended up smacking the 'iron' and getting the sack. We have heard of people making spoof phone-calls to ensure that whole days are wasted; lads placing false orders – and cancelling real orders – just to drop people in the shit; sales reps being sent on wild goose chases; and once, best of all, a salesman and raving Manchester United fan being set up with his dream appointment at Old Trafford, only to be told, by a note faxed to the reception and given to him by the club receptionist, that it was a complete wind-up.

All these may seem pathetic, childish and even dangerous, but it is worth remembering one thing. When you sit in your office telling anyone who will listen that your lads are the dog's testicles, make sure that the cup of coffee you're drinking wasn't made by someone who might possibly not agree. We have seen, on occasions too numerous to mention, how deeply people feel about the game – and if people are willing to go out and fight in defence of their club, do you really think there aren't others who will just as readily piss in your pint?

One of the beautiful things about revenge is that someone will always come up with a better method of extracting it. We received the following letter from someone who has to remain anonymous for obvious reasons, but the great thing about this one was that it was pro-English, anti-Scottish and the bloke found out about it and there was nothing he could do. Perfect.

\* \* \*

## 'ENGLISH? NO F***ING CHANCE, MATE'

A few years back, one of my best mates, Stewart, announced that he had finally decided to get married to the girl he had been living with for the previous five years. Within weeks, Blackpool had been booked for a weekend-long stag party, and now all thoughts were turning towards how we were going to stitch him up.

You know how, wherever you go in the world, you will always see some prat in a Celtic top? Well, that is the kind of bloke Stewart is. There is only one thing he hates more than Rangers and that is the England team, he is Scottish to the bone. I always find it funny how these kind of blokes end up living and working in England, if they hate the place as much as they say they do. Let alone shack up with, then end up marrying, an English Rose!

Well, Stewart has four tops to his name: Celtic, home and away, and the national side, home and away. He is a sad bastard. He lives and breathes football and, despite living in Manchester, travels up to Glasgow at least 20 times a season, as well as taking in as many games for the national side as possible. Ninety per cent of the time he is a lovely bloke but if ever we go out and he sees someone in a Rangers or England shirt, it's like a red rag to a bull. He has to say something, which very often gets him into a row where we have to try and calm things down. That can be a complete pain when it involves an England fan, because they get onto us for helping out a Sweaty instead of standing up and being English, which is fair enough. I would like to be able to say to them that he doesn't really mean it and is just pissed. But unfortunately, he really does.

Well, for the stag night there was only one thing we could do. We planned to get him totally pissed and dress him up in the England kit once he had passed out. He would go nutty when he found out. We got all the gear together and safely tucked away in one of our cases, and everything went entirely to plan. We arrived on the Friday, unpacked, and all 20 of us went straight out on the town. It was in the middle of the high season, so the place was packed and getting into a pub or a club as a stag party wasn't going to be that easy. Once we found a pub that would accept us, we decided to settle in for the duration. A couple of the lads had shot off and found a place that printed names on baseball caps, and got one made up with the words 'English through and through' printed on it.

Stewart had gone down the rack of spirits in the bar and was totally out for the count. At last orders, we carried him out up into a sideroad and did the deed. We stripped his top and trousers off and replaced them with the kit, tied his hands and feet around a lamp post and put the baseball cap firmly on his head. Then we reeled off a whole film. At first, we were going to leave him there for the police to sort out, but then decided that we should untie him and put him back in his own clothes, so that he would have no idea of what we had done until he saw the pictures.

The next day, one of the lads had the idea of getting hold of a Rangers shirt and playing the same trick, so we had a whip-round and sent someone into town to one of the local sports shops. True to form, Stewart passed out again that night, but this time we got him back to the bed-and-breakfast and put him to bed in the Rangers shirt, so that he would have a nice surprise in the morning. He went fucking mental when he woke up, and kicked up a right fuss down in the breakfast room trying to find out which bastard had done this to him. We told him that he had met a Rangers fan the night before and, despite the fact we had tried to stop him, they had acted like long-lost buddies and swapped shirts while in a drunken haze. He was gutted. You could tell he didn't really believe us, but there was enough doubt for him not to be able to blame us either.

During the next week, no one let on as to what had happened. Stewart was going out of his head expecting pictures to turn up whenever the postman came around, but we bided our time. The whole wedding went off fine, with no mention of the incident. All Stewart's relatives and mates were down from Scotland, but we still kept quiet. The happy couple were off on honeymoon the next day, so for their wedding night they were booked into a lovely countryside hotel nearby. Waiting in the room for them was a bottle of champagne, a bouquet of flowers and a homemade congratulations card from all his best mates. On the front of the card was our favourite picture of Stewart, chained up in the England kit. Apparently, he went fucking mad when he saw it and it took Jill ages to calm him down and take his mind off it. Inside the card was a message saying, 'Plenty more where that came from.' I would love to have been a fly on the wall the moment he opened it up.

By the time he came home, he had calmed down but was desperate to find out who had the photos. We kept the thing going by placing pictures in drawers all over his house for him to find when he got back home. One of the lads then told him that a picture of him in the Rangers shirt had been sent to the club, in the hope they would print it in the matchday programme. He nearly had a fit and they ended up having a punch-up in the chip shop over it. I swear, if we hadn't convinced him it was a joke, he would have gone up there and burnt down the programme printers to stop it from going out.

He is a lot better now about having a go at England fans when we're out, as he knows that he will receive a photo through the post a few days later, just to remind him. To this day, he still doesn't know who has the negatives. It would be more than my life's worth to tell him.

# PART FOUR
# South, West and Midlands

# Chapter 6
# All Quiet On The Domestic Front?

It does seem to be a strange fact of life that most of us love, or need, something to hate. It is sad, we know, but it is also true, and football provides the perfect platform for such a display of emotion.

What most fans love to hate are their local rivals and the British game contains an awful lot of local rivalries. Within this chapter, rather than look at the history of them all, which would be impossible, we have taken a very brief look around to catch the mood of a number of football fans at clubs from all levels. Most of what is contained in this chapter is violent and horrific, but we divulge it to highlight the fact that games at the lower levels are just as likely to involve violence among the supporters as any game involving one of the more infamous football firms.

You will also notice that rather than go for the obvious derby fixtures, we have picked out a few clubs who don't always merit a mention. There are a number of reasons for that. We have not included anything from the London clubs, as we covered them in *Capital Punishment*, just as the problems between the home nations were examined in *England, My England*. We have also purposely avoided writing about the so-called 'M1 derby' between Watford and L*t*n because it is too close to home (and holds too many bad memories). But the main reason why certain clubs are written about while others are not is simply because their fans wrote to us. If we are not told, we cannot know.

While we researched this book, a question kept coming back to haunt us and it is one that many fans would do well to ask themselves: what would life be like without *them*? It's a horrible thought, isn't it, and yet the more we looked, the more apparent it became that there are a number of clubs who struggle to find a true rival – and their fans find themselves in limbo, in no-man's land.

Up until 1991, Watford were the only League team in Hertfordshire. Then Barnet suddenly arrived from the Vauxhall Conference. Being in the same county and much closer to Vicarage Road than L*t*n, you might expect Barnet to give Watford fans the hump. A nice idea, but no. Watford will always hate L*t*n more than any other team, while the Bees' traditional rivals are Enfield and always will be. But it is highly unlikely that those two clubs will meet again for a fair few seasons, so will the supporters at Underhill suddenly all turn on the Hornets? And what if the Hornets were to turn their attentions from L*t*n to Barnet? Would the scum fans then turn their attentions to Northampton, who are just as close to them as we are?

Another club with a similar problem are Wycombe Wanderers. Slough Town have always been the focus for their supporters' taunting, but the chances of them meeting again are negligible, so what do they do? During the Wanderers' most recent visit to Vicarage Road, their fans started to sing that friendly old tune, 'Stand up if you hate Watford' and many joined in by lifting up their fat arses from the nice seats provided by the Watford management. This was greeted by the home fans with a chorus of, you guessed it, 'Stand up if you hate L*t*n'. If the Wycombe fans were looking to launch a new rivalry, then it didn't work. The obvious geographical choice for the Wycombe fans would be Reading or Oxford, but the latter prefer to concentrate their efforts on each other and Swindon. So Wycombe are left in limbo.

The biggest club in the country with this problem has to be Wimbledon. Due to the image of the club (or could that be Vinnie Jones), it would seem that everyone 'hates' Wimbledon in one sense, but who, exactly, are their rivals? Every other London club can easily be matched to another for their true derby fixture, but Wimbledon remain an add-on and always will. Even Crystal Palace, who share the same ground, don't really see the Dons as local rivals, preferring to unleash their animosity upon Charlton. Macclesfield Town supporters will also find themselves with the same problem as they leave their traditional rivals behind, and there lies the key. All the clubs mentioned here – Barnet, Wycombe, Wimbledon and Macclesfield – have one thing in common: they came up from the lower levels of the game only recently. And as we all know, local rivalries are bred into supporters. Not chosen, but traditional.

There is, however, one interesting exception to that rule. Hereford United recently went the other way and left the Nationwide League, although it wasn't without a fight. Stuck in the middle of nowhere, the Hereford fans find themselves in an unusual situation because they have no truly 'local' derby to look forward to. However, any thoughts you might have of Hereford being a quiet backwater may need a bit of revision. Rob provided us with the lowdown on a group of fans who have seen their fair share of trouble over the years.

## HEREFORD

What's really annoying about following United is our location. Shrewsbury is 50 miles north, Birmingham 50 miles north-east, Bristol 50 miles south and Cardiff 50 miles south-west. I would also like to put the record straight: Hereford are as much English as the George Cross. All those twats that call us Welsh whenever we play them ought to have paid a bit of attention in their geography classes – at least *we* know the shape of *our* country. Hereford is 20 miles from the Welsh border. I'll say that again, for all the thick northerners – Wales is fucking 20 miles away, OK!

It is so amusing when 'no mob' Chester and Shrewsbury call us 'sheep-shaggers'. Half the Chester ground is in Wales and Shrewsbury is as close to the border as we are. We hate the fucking Welsh as much as they hate us, and they swarm over the border to have a pop at us whenever they get the chance. Still, it keeps it exciting. You see, we get it from all angles.

At United, there were two crews really: the Dresser Crew, all Fila, Ellesse, Pringle, etc, and another group of around 15–20 blokes who never used a name. These lads were older and harder. They were also more organised and used to travel using various methods so as not to attract the attention of the police. They used to take the piss out of the Dresser lads in their 'nice' clothes – but when it went off, they were all in it together.

Our deadly rivals were Newport County, before they bottled out of the League. So now it's Cardiff. Let's be honest here, Cardiff are very tidy. They outnumber us every time. We do our best and win the odd battle, but we would never win that war. If Cardiff were ever to do anything football-wise, and I think not, then they would be a match for anyone in the country. But at least we can hold our heads up about going down to their place and not bottling it.

Going down to Bristol is always a bit of a laugh. When we played City in the Freight Rover Trophy area final a few years back, we travelled down in a convoy of transit vans. We had been on an all-dayer, as this was a big match for us and everyone and his dog was out. As we drove through Tintern on the way down, the lads in the front were mucking about by hanging out of the windows of the vans and shouting at everyone we passed. Being pissed, I decided to climb out of the window and onto the roof for a bit of 'surfing'. We travelled for miles with me on the roof, when I suddenly spotted a police car waiting up ahead, waving the van down. I dived back in through the window, hoping to escape, when an ambulance pulled up alongside and the driver pointed me out. I had been posing, thinking that all the vans behind us were full of our lads. Unfortunately, the ambulance was tucked in just three vans back and the driver had phoned the police 'for my own safety'. I was arrested and missed the biggest game in years.

Wrexham is another top game for us. They have fuck-all boys up there. Lots of verbal and plenty of runners, that's Wrexham. The England–Wales bit makes this a bit of a derby for us, despite the distance. The 1977–78 season games were good ones. Up there, we were following the club coaches up when the police turned up to give them an escort to the ground. We hung back a bit in our transit and noticed this gang of lads giving the mums and dads on the coaches loads of abuse. The police let them get on with it, but we pulled over and waited until the coaches were out of sight and the police were nowhere to be seen. We then pulled up alongside them as they were laughing and acting all laddo. They ran like fuck when we jumped out, but we managed to catch one lad and threw him in the back of the transit. He was shitting himself as we took the piss and scared the life out of him. We drove him to the middle of nowhere, stripped him naked, tied him up and chucked him in the bushes. I often wonder what happened to the poor sod. Imagine having to live with that for the rest of your life.

For the return game at our place, Wrexham brought loads down. The match was played towards the end of the season. They were going well and looking for promotion, while we were on our way down and playing shit. With most of the teams who would bring that many fans, you would feel a bit apprehensive and expect them to have a good pop at your end or the local pubs, but not Wrexham. It just meant there were more to go round for all the United lads. Five minutes before kick-off, two lads ran onto the pitch from the Meadow End (the Hereford home terrace) decked out from head to toe in Wrexham gear. Cheeky fuckers, so most of the fans thought. The Wrexham fans gave them a huge cheer, as their 'heroes' had had the bottle to front the Hereford fans in their own end. When the two lads reached the centre spot, they stopped and pulled off the shite red-and-white kit and started to wipe their arses on it, before throwing it on the ground and stamping it into the mud. It was fucking hilarious. The Wrexham fans zipped up straight away, while the rest of the ground cracked up laughing. The kit they were wearing had been made up from the result of turning over some of the Welsh wankers before the game. Talk about rubbing it in!

The two lads then ran back to the Meadow End, avoided the police and managed to mingle in with the rest of the crowd and not get arrested. It was one of those things you wish you had had the bottle to do. What a story to tell your kids about.

One story I must tell you is about our FA Cup visit to Spurs a few years back. Now, I know it's not a derby game, but as I've said before, every club looks at us as being in the middle of nowhere and therefore supported by village idiots who come from incestuous families. On this occasion, even I must admit that the first part of that did seem possible.

As normal for a big game, we ran our own bus. Again we had started early and by the time we got to London I was totally slaughtered and had passed out. The bus had stopped at Tottenham Court Road so that the lads could have a tour of the pubs in the West End before making their own way up to White Hart Lane. I wouldn't move an inch, so the lads told the driver to take me up to the ground on my own and let me sleep it off, and told him to tell me they would meet me at the match.

I eventually woke up some two hours before kick-off. I was still feeling shit-faced, but decided to leave the bus and walk up the Tottenham High Road and find a cafe or something to eat. As I made my way past the locals, I could see them laughing and smirking at me as they went. I thought they were taking the piss out of the way I was staggering about, so I gave them the benefit of the doubt and let it go. I finally caught the smell of a burger van and my stomach took over the control of my legs and headed in the general direction of the 'food'.

Before I ordered, the bloke behind the counter said in his chirpy, Cockney manner, 'You look nice and colourful today, son.' I thought, well, I must look a bit pale from all the booze, but I didn't think that this twat was that funny, really, so I gave him a sarcastic grin and ordered a burger. As I waited, this lad wearing a Hereford top comes up behind me. On seeing the shirt, I start to make conversation but he stops me and says, 'Nice face-painting job you have there, mate.' Not another piss-taker, I thought, and one of my own kind as well. I staggered away as the two stood there laughing. 'I'd take a look in a mirror if I were you, son,' shouted the burger man. 'Fuck off,' I replied. I must admit, curiosity had now taken me over. What the fuck were they on about? Then I stopped and took a look in a car mirror. My bastard mates on the bus had given me a full face-painting job while I was out cold. For the last half hour, I had been walking around the Spurs heartland with 'Tottenham wankers', 'Cockneys are shitters' and all sorts of things guaranteed to get me a good hiding. The 'village idiot' tag was probably all that saved me.

The main 'known' firm to follow Hereford United, the Dresser Crew, took their name from the pride they had in wearing the designer labels associated with the casual movement. Although the hard core of the group only totalled between 20 and 30 lads, they caused plenty of problems for the police throughout the country and are well worth a brief examination.

The FA Cup has seen them at their worst. In 1982, 29 fans,

not all Hereford supporters, were arrested when Leicester City came to play. The visiting coaches were ambushed and fighting broke out throughout the city. Another incident took place in 1985, when Hereford were drawn to play at Yeovil. Fighting in the town before the game involved a group estimated by the police to number approximately 100 Hereford supporters. The fighting continued in the ground as the Hereford fans invaded the pitch. One youth was stopped just in the nick of time as he went to attack the Yeovil manager, Gerry Gow, with a glass. Following the game, the Yeovil fans attacked the Hereford supporters' coaches, causing £800 worth of damage. The violence surrounding the match was so bad that Yeovil threatened to ban all away fans for FA Cup matches.

Before the FA Cup tie at Yeovil, the Hereford fans had travelled to Reading for a league fixture. Following trouble in various pubs before the game, the home fans decided to take revenge and infiltrate the away end. Fighting on a scale that is, thankfully, rarely seen nowadays saw a running terrace battle as both sets of fans tried to gain the upper hand. The half-time whistle was almost due before the police finally restored order.

In 1990, Manchester United came to play at Edgar Street. This was seen by the locals as an ideal opportunity to 'put the word out' that Hereford were not to be seen as an easy touch by anyone. Man United fans were ambushed in the Kerry Arms pub by a gang using knives, broken pool-cues, pool balls and broken glasses, resulting in many fans needing hospital treatment. Following this incident, Hereford became what many saw as an unlikely target for police raids, as the authorities tried to clamp down on organised football violence. In November 1990, under the title of 'Operation Mars', the police raided houses in Leeds, Norwich, Liverpool, Sheffield, Newcastle and Manchester, as well as Hereford. Just prior to this, 28 supporters had been arrested following violence during a fixture with Cardiff City. Again, not all those arrested were Hereford fans.

The police operation clearly didn't deter those intent on

causing trouble as just one year later, they were at it again. During an away tie at non-league Atherstone, the police had to call in special support units to assist the 60 officers they already had on duty. Over 100 fans clashed continually as eye witnesses reported the use of broom handles, spades and even a pitchfork among the usual array of weaponry. The police came in for criticism from some fans as it was reported that in order to gain control, they had allowed the dog handlers to release their animals and let them run wild. Others reported that the police had had no alternative, if they were to restore any kind of order. Over 20 people were treated in hospital following the violence at this game.

It was, of course, not only in the Cup competitions that the violence occurred. In March 1981, 56 arrests were made following 'the worst outbreak of violence the city had seen' when Hereford played host to Newport County. This was an extension of the trouble that had followed a League Cup meeting between the two earlier in the season. Further disorder occurred at Chester, Bristol and Blackpool. Before an away game at Plymouth, a local pub was wrecked, leading the police to call for reinforcements and a helicopter to monitor the movements of a certain group. The club's supporters found themselves banned from the away game at Torquay in the 1986–87 season, following the violence that took place during their previous meeting at Plainmoor, where seats were ripped out and thrown onto the pitch.

The unhappy story goes on, but just as it seemed that the club had shaken off the hooligans, they came out of the woodwork once again. An attempt to ambush the Burnley firm known as the Suicide Squad was a clear message that they still craved recognition. The pub used by the Burnley fans was attacked, with glasses being thrown. A police dog handler needed stitches for a head wound he received, and homemade knives were found discarded at the scene. As recently as January 1996, the police intelligence unit were at Edgar Street monitoring the movements of the fans at an FA Cup tie against Tottenham. (This may have had something to do with the fact that fans from both clubs were known to follow the national side, and the police were busy collecting as much information as possible during the pre-Euro 96 period.) Just for the cameras, and the police helicopter flying overhead, the hooligans provided them with something to look at, as fighting broke out in the ground and afterwards outside.

Hereford may not have a local derby; they may not even be in the Football League at the present time; but rest assured that their hooligans' exploits continue and they should be treated with the utmost caution.

Now, think about it again, what would you do without *your* local rivals? Hate them though we do, maybe we should be thankful that we have them.

# Chapter 7
# The Local Scene

Of all the derby fixtures within the British game, it is often the unlikeliest ones which produce the most hatred and violence. The Bristol derby, which we will look at later, is a classic example of this. What should, to the neutral outsider at least, simply be a passionate regional affair has instead become an almost guaranteed banker when it comes to witnessing hooliganism, often on a huge and terrifying scale. Cardiff v Swansea is another such fixture, as has been seen on far too many occasions. You could even say the same about Reading v Oxford.

Another game which confirms the existence of this phenomenon takes place down on the south coast. Portsmouth have always been known for having a large and volatile following, but the hostility exhibited by their infamous 657 Crew towards their local rivals Southampton at times almost beggars belief. Indeed, it was once remarked to us that it borders on insanity.

What follows is an examination of that rivalry dating back to the 1970s. It was put together and given to us by someone who is best kept anonymous and adapted from our interview with him and other information we have received on this local hostility. Admittedly, what follows is written from the Pompey viewpoint, but it is, nevertheless, a real eye-opener.

## *POMPEY*

Like most supporters, we refer to our local rivals as 'the scum', or in our case, 'Scumhampton'. Over the last few seasons, the Scumhampton supporters have started calling us 'scummers', although it used to be 'skates', for some reason.

It isn't just with them, either. If some half-wit club like Reading come down with an ex-scummer in their side, then we're all for giving him a good hiding as well. It isn't just a rivalry with these; it's pure and utter hatred for anything to do with them.

For the record, the first thing I ever heard about the rivalry between the two clubs was back in the 1969–70 season. The two sides played a 'friendly' at The Dell on behalf of an ex-scum player called John Siddonen. There was trouble before the game, and inside the ground the Pompey lads took over half of the Milton Terrace, which at that time was the scummers' end. A smoke bomb and loads of bottles were thrown as the Pompey lads got a right result. Although the actual match finished at 9.30, fighting was still going on at 10.15 and during this trouble, two people were put in hospital, while the police made seven arrests on the night. That same season, Everton played at The Dell in a game that became infamous for the trouble caused by a large group of Portsmouth fans, passing through Southampton and fighting with both Everton and Saints fans.

During the 1972–73 season, Pompey were at home to Aston Villa and a group of about 100 Southampton fans, instead of going to Birmingham, went to Fratton Park. This led to a massive confrontation in a road that was to become a frequent battleground for the two sets of fans, Goldsmith Avenue.

Two seasons later, when the two teams met at The Dell, 315 Pompey fans were arrested on arrival in the city and made to sit in an exercise yard until they were charged, after they had totally wrecked a train bringing them to Southampton. Pompey fans again made their way into the Milton End, where, during yet more disturbances, one fan was taken to hospital with a suspected broken collarbone. There were 14 arrests and 60 ejections during this one game, which became even more infamous when the referee, Clive Thomas, was attacked by a Southampton supporter.

When the two teams met for the return fixture at Fratton Park, there were more disturbances, with the Southampton fans once again getting the worst of the deal.

The following season, 1975–76, the fixture at The Dell saw the largest contingent of policemen ever to patrol the city on the day of a match (up to that point), 230 uniformed officers. However, as luck would have it, heavy rain kept most people away from the city centre, although there was still the odd bit of trouble. Then, 14 minutes from the end of the game and immediately after Southampton had scored their fourth goal, 400 Pompey supporters surged from the Archers Road end of the ground. Despite the driving rain, they ran towards the centre of the city, fighting with each other as they ran. They smashed numerous windows in houses, shops and business premises, but they were eventually subdued by the police, who turned them back towards Central railway station. There was also fighting in local bus stations and police had to break up two gangs outside the Royal Hotel who were fighting with chains. A local resident was attacked and suffered a black eye when he attempted to stop a group of Portsmouth fans from urinating in his front garden. In all, despite the heavy police presence, there were 22 arrests, four of which were for assaults on policemen.

Prior to the 1978–79 season, Pompey were at home to Chelsea in a friendly and during the inevitable trouble between those two sets of fans, mainly between the ground and Fratton station, the police arrested 27 supporters. However, a strange incident took place on the 5.35 Fratton to Southampton train, when a small group of nine Southampton supporters, who had gone to the game to support Chelsea(!), attacked four Portsmouth supporters. The two groups had been chanting abuse at each other during the journey but when the train pulled into Fareham station, fighting broke out in the carriage and quickly spilled out onto the platform. During that trouble, a 17-year-old Pompey fan was kicked onto the railtrack and fell under the wheels of the train. As a result of this, his right leg was crushed and seven days later, surgeons were forced to amputate the leg.

The problems continued, although not always involving actual violence. Early on in the eighties, the Pompey fans had hit upon the 'novel' idea of bombing the Southampton coaches with blue paint as they travelled either past or through the city on their way to fixtures with Brighton. Quite simply, as the coaches passed under bridges, paint would be tipped onto the roofs and, if they were 'lucky', over the windows. This became a regular occurrence and a mighty pain in the arse for the coach operators but it was difficult to deal with, as the police could hardly patrol every bridge between Southampton and Portsmouth.

Although trouble between the two sets of fans had been ever present, the 1983–84 season, the so-called 'year of the casual', saw the violence return with a new ferocity that even astonished many of those who took part. The game in question was a fourth round FA Cup tie at Fratton Park. Even before the match, two mobs, each around 250–300 strong, battled it out in Goldsmith Avenue. Early casualties of the fighting included a 21-year-old Portsmouth fan, who was attacked and slashed across the eye on his way to the ground, and a policeman, who was also taken to hospital with a broken hand.

Inside Fratton Park, coins and other missiles were

thrown, but of more serious importance was the fact that a number of Portsmouth fans on the South Terrace had managed to sneak wire-cutters into the ground and were caught attempting to cut through the fence to get at the Southampton supporters. At the end of the game, following another late goal and subsequent victory for Southampton, the Portsmouth fans realised they could not get to the Southampton fans due to their heavy escort, and so around 1,000 of them attacked the police. Policemen in riot gear were deployed to quell the trouble on Fratton Bridge, but around 60 shop windows were put through in Fratton Road and two pubs were 'totalled'. Despite 350 policemen being on duty, six police vehicles were badly damaged, 59 people were arrested, 32 were ejected from the ground and over £8,000 worth of damage was done to local shops.

That same season, a funfair on Southampton Common was the scene of more fighting. Fifty Pompey lads turned up and went through the fair, ending up battling with a group of approximately 50 Southampton lads. One youth was stabbed with a knife and a total of 50 police were deployed to remove the Pompey lads and escort them all the way back to Portsmouth.

The 1985–86 season saw another strange incident, during the Southampton reserves v Portsmouth reserves fixture. Portsmouth's league game had been postponed and so a group of approximately 100 lads travelled to The Dell to watch the reserves play. As they left the ground, they were ambushed by a large group of Southampton fans, but the fighting soon spread and extra police were deployed to control the trouble, which continued all the way back to Central station.

That same season, Southampton met Millwall in an FA Cup fifth round tie at The Dell. This game was to see yet more problems involving Pompey (who, it has to be said, are hardly fans of Millwall either). A large police presence was keeping a watchful eye on the Millwall supporters, but a number of the 657 Crew had been to The Dell and bought tickets during the week. About 60 of them were in the East Stand and soon began brawling with Southampton supporters in that area, and then with Millwall. Trouble continued during the game and then again afterwards, and of the 28 fans arrested on the day, 15 were from Pompey.

More trouble erupted the following season, 1986–87, but this time well away from The Dell or Fratton Park and, more importantly, away from the watchful eyes of the police. Flemming Park in Eastleigh – a borough of Southampton – was the ground allocated for a Sunday league cup tie between two pub sides, the Tabbycat and the Air Balloon. The Air Balloon was known for being one of the 657 Crew's main pubs at that time and a number of their main lads were thought to be in the side. A groundsman at the park reportedly saw a number of lads arrive for the match with a large bag of tools and during the match, about 20 of the Southampton firm the Inside Crew arrived, armed with hammers and baseball bats. They attacked the supporters before invading the pitch and attacking the Air Balloon players. The referee took the players off the pitch and they all retreated to the safety of the changing-rooms. By the time the police arrived, the fighting was over but one of the Air Balloon players was semi-conscious, one had a broken hand and another had reportedly been stabbed. However, not only did those injured refuse to make a complaint, they also refused to go to hospital as well. Despite this, the subsequent police investigation saw three Southampton fans arrested and charged.

That same season, The Dell staged an FA Trophy fixture between Fareham and Kidderminster. The 657 Crew allegedly attended the match to confront the Inside Crew, who were also present, but although there were eight arrests and 15 ejections, police managed to avert any serious trouble and reported only minor scuffles.

The following season, 1987–88, Pompey had won promotion and, four games in, played Southampton at Fratton Park. With almost 400 officers on duty and, for the first time, the Optica spotter plane at their disposal, the police were convinced that they would be able to track the fans' movements and keep on top of any trouble. However, at around midday, the first of a number of serious incidents took place. In the first, a 21-year-old Pompey fan was slashed across the face with a stanley knife. Another was slashed across the chin, while a third was attacked and received minor stab wounds. In the Goldsmith Avenue area, a major fight broke out when 300 Portsmouth supporters chased an equal number of Saints fans down the narrow streets of Apsley Road and Claydon Avenue, right next to the ground. At full-time, the Pompey fans tried to attack the Southampton supporters on the corner of the North Terrace as they were leaving the ground. Dozens of Pompey fans were reported as climbing over the fences from the North Stand, but they were held back by 20 policemen, all with truncheons drawn. The group then kicked over a garden wall and began pelting the police with the rubble, while making – it was reported in the local press – loud and offensive monkey noises. After about 10 minutes, the Pompey fans began fighting with the police who had provided a huge escort for the Southampton supporters moving back to Fratton station. It was during this period that two distress flares were fired at policemen from within the ranks of the Pompey fans. The fighting continued in the backstreets off Goldsmith Avenue right through until 7.30 that night, by which time 56 people had been arrested, 42 of whom were from Portsmouth.

For the return fixture at The Dell that same season, the Portsmouth supporters put the word out that they were really going to do the business on the scummers, and for a game with a 12 o'clock kick-off, that would mean an early start. Up to 500 policemen were on duty for the game and they had set up a number of roadblocks to check every vehicle coming into the city. However, a large group of the 657 Crew had planned to evade the police at Central station by getting off early at St Denys. Although they initially managed to get through the small police presence on the approach road to the station, a fleet of riot vans arrived and managed to get hold of them. By 9.40 in the morning, this group of 103 Pompey fans had been detained.

During the 1989–90 season, Portsmouth were drawn away to Crystal Palace in an FA Cup third round tie on the same day that Southampton were drawn to play at Tottenham. As expected, the two sets of fans arranged to take their feud into London and by 12.45, over 100 of them were fighting in the Nag's Head pub in James Street, Covent Garden. A canister of CS gas was let off, over 50 glasses were smashed and missiles thrown through windows before the violence spilt out into the street. The two gangs, by now armed with chains, bottles and bar stools, fought a pitched battle until the police arrived and forced them apart. As a result of this fight, there were a number of serious hospital cases, but the police also confiscated a large number of CS gas canisters from other fans. Despite this, the fighting restarted in a nearby street when over 60 fans threw ashtrays at each other. After their respective games, the two sets of fans returned to Covent Garden, where it had been arranged to meet up again. This time, over 200 supporters left the streets littered with broken glass. Trouble had also broken out at Waterloo station soon after the games had finished, but as the police moved the supporters down from Covent Garden, more fights broke out and these continued right up until almost 10 o'clock. More fighting occurred on trains heading south and resulted in 13 arrests at various stations en route. Indeed, at one point it became so bad that a train was stopped on the way to Winchester so that police could contain the trouble.

In 1992, Southampton made it to Wembley for the Zenith Data Systems Cup final, where, thankfully, they were beaten. However, the Pompey fans could not let such a day pass without incident and as Southampton fans travelled up the M3, they found a number of Pompey supporters at a service station, where numerous fights broke out. Later on, when word got out, the Saints firm arrived at the service station in force and the Pompey lads were given a serious kicking for their trouble. After the game, at least two car-loads of Pompey lads were to be found driving round Southampton, dishing out hidings to anyone foolish enough to be wearing colours. In one particularly bad attack, two teenagers were beaten with hammers as they stepped off a club coach.

Following this, there were no major incidents between the two sets of supporters until the 1993–94 season, when Southampton travelled to Fratton Park for Alan Knight's testimonial game. A crowd of around 17,000 saw no trouble before or during the game, but afterwards, a group of around 300 Pompey fans tried to attack the Southampton supporters as they left the ground. When the police intervened, the Pompey fans fought running battles with them, during which time more walls were dismantled, a number of police cars were attacked and yet another distress flare was fired at the police. But the most serious incident took place when a police van was attacked by Pompey fans throwing missiles who then ran into the Froddington Arms pub. Around 40 policemen then charged into the pub, attacking all those inside with batons. It resulted in a number of serious allegations being made against the police, all of which were subsequently dropped. Disturbances connected with this game took place as far afield as Eastleigh and Fareham – right on the fringes of the two cities – and continued right up until 11 o'clock. But despite this, and the fact that one policeman was in hospital after being seriously assaulted, the police made only three arrests in the entire day.

The 1995–96 season saw another Cup tie between the two clubs and more trouble between the two sets of fans. Although the police maintained a very high profile, a 3–0 victory for the scummers saw the Pompey fans in vindictive mood, and a group of them managed to get through the cordon and attack the Southampton supporters with traffic cones and bricks. It was also rumoured that a pre-arranged 'off' in the city centre saw 80 Southampton fans turn up to take on a group of 30 Pompey fans, but the Pompey ran them ragged before the police managed to get a grip on them and get them out of harm's way.

Recent contrasting fortunes have seen the clubs meet all too infrequently for the liking of the Pompey fans, as the mood between the supporters is one of real outright hatred. A hatred that can only be compared to Millwall and West Ham in its intensity, and one that has to be experienced to be believed.

# Chapter 8

# Way Out West

Bristol is not the first city that springs to mind when the words 'a football hotbed' are mentioned. Indeed, you do sometimes get the impression that as far as the media are concerned, the only team in the west is Chelsea! Well, if ever proof were needed that passions do run high for the supporters of 'little' clubs, then Sky Television provided it with a bang in December 1996 by beaming the Bristol derby live throughout the country.

I. and H. provide the Blue view from a city divided and in serious trouble.

## A HEAD FULL OF GAS

'Football returned to the dark days' was how one local newspaper chose to describe the events at Ashton Gate on 16 December 1996. As the celebrating Rovers fans spilled onto the pitch following their last-minute equaliser, the City fans went for the kill. The police finally cleared the pitch, the final whistle went and the mob returned. This time more of them, and going after the players. Then, not content with that, they came back towards us and in to our end, hitting out at old men and throwing missiles at families, leaving one woman unconscious. Very macho. The words 'disgraceful scenes' were used by the commentators at least 10 times as they focused in to catch every last punch and beam it across the watching nation, sparking varying degrees of outrage. To Gasheads (Rovers fans), these scenes were not really a surprise, not really anything new; just a little more 'in your face' maybe. In the corresponding fixture the year before, two more goals by Peter Beadle had caused a similar reaction among the meatheads in that very same area. On that occasion, the advertising boards had thwarted them so they resorted to tearing up their own ground rather than the opposing fans. Oh, how they must love their club. You see, the 'dark days' that the local hacks referred to had never really gone away.

A brief resumé of the last 10 years gives an idea of the almost sectarian nature of the problem facing this particular local derby. In March 1989, for example, a 1–1 draw at Twerton Park was followed by a baseball-bat attack on a renowned City pub in the heart of Rovers territory. A whole set of tit-for-tat attacks ensued over the remainder of the season, leading to a grudge Sunday morning pub match having to be abandoned due to crowd trouble.

The culmination of the 'Bristol double' season came on the glorious night of 2 May 1990, when Rovers dismantled City 3–0 to snatch the title from under the noses of the Reds. The City fans tried to make up for their team's disgraceful showing by attempting to pull the ground apart and throwing advertising hoardings onto the pitch. The damage done that night was nothing compared to what happened a few months later, when a group of meatheads on their way back from West Brom decided they would stop off in Bath and set fire to Twerton Park. Not being the brightest of souls, the arsonists were caught red-handed within five miles of the blaze. Inevitably, their names and addresses were made public at the subsequent court case, and it doesn't take too much to work out what happened as a result of that.

The local constabulary were no doubt delighted when

Rovers were relegated in 1993 – courtesy of a certain Malcolm Allison – but following City's own inevitable relegation, the derby was now back on. Not surprisingly, all the old hostilities have returned as well, and with a vengeance. The two matches at Ashton Gate are cases in point, but some of the events away from the games wouldn't look out of place in Bosnia. A family living in the south of Bristol were forced to leave the area after prolonged abuse and harassment ended in the 'execution' of their two cats following City's play-off elimination by Brentford.

The times of the 1950s when the Bristol City Robin would face up to the Bristol Rovers Pirate in front of a good-natured crowd are long past. Now, hatred is the order of the day. Part of the reason for this conflict probably lies in the outlook and expectations of the two clubs, as the contrast between the two could hardly be greater. Talk to a City fan for more than two minutes and you can guarantee they will mention two things. One, the fact that they have been in the top division; and two, that they have a ground fit for the top division. In their eyes, they are a 'big' club.

To us Gasheads, City are a joke. Yes, they were in the top flight, for four seasons in the late seventies. Then they went down . . . and down . . . and down, all the way from top to bottom in consecutive seasons before finally going bust. Happy days for Gasheads throughout the globe. Miraculously, they reappeared with '1982' after their name. Amazingly, in the 15 years since their resurrection, the fans, along with the board, have somehow managed to convince themselves that they are – that old chestnut – 'a sleeping giant'. Unfortunately, a couple of Freight Rover Trophy appearances and a runners-up slot in the Third Division (yes, I said runners-up slot) don't really justify the tag. A comatose elephant would be much closer to the reality of the situation they currently find themselves in.

As for Ashton Gate, well, for Rovers fans that conjures up memories of the famous *Not The Nine O'Clock News* comedy spoof of the Fiat car advertisements: 'Designed by computer, assembled with the latest technology and run by morons.' Is there any other club in the country that would lock its own season-ticket holders out of the derby fixture, as apparently happened in the 1995–96 season? The first derby for three years, and about 5,000 people were locked outside. It was all quite comical to us, until you heard about the gates being stormed, the outbreak of crowd violence and the woman steward who had her leg broken. Amazingly, no fine was forthcoming from the FA, letting Bristol City off the hook and in profit at the expense of others.

It's probably very simplistic, but I'll say it anyway: is it any coincidence that every major incident of note on the Bristol hooligan front during the course of the nineties seems to have stemmed from one thing – the 'big', 'glamorous' club, with lots of 'potential' (apparently) and a 'Premiership-standard stadium', being brought to its knees by the tinpot team with no ground of its own that has to survive on a shoestring? I think not.

The simple truth is that City are a big club in all but one thing: results. Rovers fans expect a lot less and have the ability to laugh at themselves. It's significant that despite losing their last two home derbies, the Rovers fans have not attempted to rip up their own ground, invade the pitch or attack the opposition players, as their southern counterparts have! Forty fans were arrested following the trouble in December; only two were Rovers fans! It remains to be seen if the police action has had any effect on the tribalistic attitude that seems to take over the majority when the two clash.

One thing is certain, though: if things continue as they are now, then we will find ourselves saddled with the same situation they face over the border at the Cardiff–Swansea matches, where away fans are banned altogether. That situation is closer than most will admit. Already we are at the stage where only 'nice' City fans were 'invited' to buy tickets for the return match at the Memorial Ground. Those supporters were then shuttled to the stadium under the strictest security and their names and addresses were kept on record, 'just in case'. The exercise had limited success. Some tickets found their way into the wrong hands, leading to a disturbance when City scored. Rovers also did not monitor the sponsorship and hospitality ticket-sales closely enough (well, you can't upset the suit-and-tie brigade, can you?), which provoked further skirmishes in the stands.

Overall, 11 arrests were made. Not too bad considering the tensions bubbling over from the previous encounter, but still 11 too many. The reaction of the crowd towards these morons was encouraging, to say the least, but both clubs would be naive to think that one game signals the start of a new era. Especially when it was played on a Sunday lunchtime, amid Fort Knox-style security and with a specially invited set of away fans.

Now, below, John expresses his view. It may come from the Red half of the city, but it would seem that there are a few that can at least agree on something.

## TWO TEAMS IN BRISTOL

Bristol, a huge, sprawling city in this forgotten part of the country, has somehow always managed to under-achieve. With a reported crime rate among the worst in the country, it has become a violent place. There are parts of the city that are no-go places for its people and even more dangerous for the police to enter. A reflection, possibly, of the fact that like the city, many of its people have also underachieved.

It is a sad admission that the major sporting event in this part of the world is a mid-table clash between two very ordinary Second Division sides. A sadder reflection, still, is the importance the people of the West Country place on the fixture. I think it is fair to say that a city this size deserves a better football team, but no club in the world deserves the kind of support that turns out when the two sides meet. Football has always provided people with an opportunity to taste some kind of success, a chance to become a winner at least once a week. In a city divided, that success becomes all the more important.

Over the years, the fixture has sadly been saddled with increasing violence. City have a much larger fan-base than their neighbours and the violence has mainly been instigated by their followers. It must be said, though, that the fans wearing blue are no angels them-selves and have also had their moments during the increasing battle.

The move to Bath did nothing to quell the fighting. Indeed, in some ways it was seen as a victory, as Rovers had been forced to leave the city. Now, for one set of fans, there really was 'only one team in Bristol' and that was how it should always remain. The attempt to burn down the stadium by a gang of City fans was seen as an attempt to finally push Rovers out of business. Thankfully, it failed. The gang became known as the 'City Fire Brigade' and even had T-shirts printed with a photograph of the burnt-out stands on it. These could be seen openly at City matches following the arson attack. Nice.

Despite the lack of success enjoyed by either club, the fixture has become bigger and bigger. Some would argue that this is purely due to their failure, as being champions of the city is all either side can realistically hope for come the end of the season. This growing importance showed itself when too many tickets were sold for the match at Ashton Gate the year before last. There were 22,000 inside, with another estimated 3,000 ticket-holders locked out. Inevitably, trouble flared, leaving the police stretched to the limit.

In 1996, Rovers returned to the city, taking up residence with the rugby club at the Memorial Ground. The battle for the city was back on, and the papers loved it. The local press and regional television have always come down in favour of the Robins, and in some cases, the return of Rovers was treated more in the fashion of an unwanted relative coming to stay, rather than a welcome back home for the city's other team.

The fixture lists were released and Ashton Gate was to be the venue for the first big clash following Rovers' return to the city. As the match drew near, Sky Television decided to take the game and screen it live into the living-rooms and pubs of Britain. This was to prove a big mistake. The local media built the tie up in an unbelievable manner. City were firmly installed as favourites to win 'the biggest game for years' (mid-table Second Division, remember). Expectations were fuelled – 'seven days to go' – as countdown commenced. The local paper finally printed an eight-page pull-out on the day prior to the match, turning anything less than victory into a total disaster for the home fans.

Rumours of violence were rife, as certain elements had planned a less-than-warm welcome for the visiting fans. Rovers returned over 1,500 tickets, as some felt the safety of their own front rooms to be a much better option. Warnings like these surely wouldn't go unnoticed by the police, or those in charge at Ashton Gate, and many believed that a large police presence would have to be in place to protect those that did attend. However, the trouble had started well before kick-off; pubs were attacked, cars and buses had windows smashed, people were getting punched in the street. Madness. The police were stretched to the limit but what could they do? It's impossible to police every street corner. In the stadium, however, things should have been very different.

Trouble was erupting throughout the match and the danger areas were easy to spot. As always, the main bulk of the hooligans were gathered in the same areas of the stadium. Despite what the club, the press and the police were to claim later, many of the same old faces appeared intent on playing their part in what was to follow. Football clubs, in order to cut policing costs, are placing more responsibility on the role that their stewards have to play, but surely placing office workers, students and house-wives in such a dangerous situation is beyond the call of duty. These people are being paid to show supporters to their seats, not to stop a riot. The main bulk of the hooligans numbered around 500 and it quickly became clear that the police were about to fight a losing battle. Many more should have been brought in before it became too late.

When Beadle scored Rovers' last-minute equaliser, over 300 hooligans invaded the pitch as fighting broke out between the rival supporters. The police did their best and did it well, but when the final whistle went, they had no chance. It wasn't from just that end of the stadium that the hooligans then came. As the police tried to keep the rival fans apart, the players came under attack.

The officer in charge of policing the fixture, despite what had been seen by the television viewers, claimed after the fixture that the 150 officers he had on duty were sufficient for the match. It was also suggested that pre-planned violence on this scale was hard to contain, really. Was this an admission of prior knowledge? If so, he clearly got his numbers and his tactics wrong.

Following the match, City stated that these people were not regular fans, they were the type that only turn out when violence is likely, and the Rovers administration backed them up. Even the local press went along with this line and claimed never to have seen any of these people before! Where do they come from, Mars? I've watched the footage over and over; I don't know the names, but I know the faces. I've seen them before, indulging in their activities, home and away. I saw people run past me from 10 rows back in order to join in, people that go week in, week out. City fans through and through, caught up in the frenzy. Did I go with them? Well, thankfully, no – but it was close. Just how far in our personal lives have we fallen when victory over our neighbour becomes so important, so absolutely vital? The media, those involved at both clubs and the fans themselves have, for this particular fixture, replaced their support with nothing more than pure hatred.

For the return fixture at the Memorial Ground, security was tightened. Due to the stadium's capacity, the allocated number of away fans was considerably less than for the match at Ashton Gate, and this should have made the job for the police and the clubs so much easier. Under tight security, the police only allowed those City supporters with tickets to travel to the match, on official coaches, and during their stay, they were kept well away from the home fans and surrounded at all times. City had been very careful in allocating the tickets and the press had played their part this time in playing down the fixture, yet somehow you still felt that something would go wrong.

Somehow, 30 or so City fans had managed to get tickets and infiltrate a section of the stadium mainly occupied by families. As most of us have witnessed at some stage, these people are not too fussy about whom they attack, as long as they attack someone other than their own. The police moved in, as did some of the home fans, and terrace warfare was with us once more. The vast majority booed and jeered as those involved were escorted away, and I began to wonder if we would ever rid our game from such scum. I blamed Rovers, City, the police, the local press, the Football Association, anyone other than myself. Then I asked what role, if any, I could play? As the local 'heroes' got closer, I once again recognised a few of the old faces, faces I could have pointed out after watching the video from the last fixture. If, just if, we all came together and stood up to these people once and for all, en masse, then they would be gone, banned. Unless we change our ways soon, we could find our two football stadiums turn out to be just like other parts of the city, no-go areas for certain kinds of people.

I honestly believe that both clubs have been seriously at fault in the past, as have the police, but if we, as fans, finally show a willingness to help, then we may just crack it. So here we go, form an orderly queue over there, please. Eh, after you, mate.

No, I insist.

For most who watch the game courtesy of Sky, the Bristol derby provided them with a type of entertainment they were hardly expecting. Funnily enough, those of us who actually bother to go might well have been able to warn them. Simon wrote to us with his views on the day:

## SAFE, AT LEAST FOR NOW

Ninety minutes are up and the referee has the whistle to his lips. Twenty thousand people are waiting to celebrate their great moment. Already the taunts rain thick, fast and ugly, showering down on the supporters – the scum – of their local rivals. There has already been trouble. We have already seen the mighty surge at the mums and dads, at the old boys and the children. The brave soldiers of the Red Army, ready to take on all who enter their domain, be they 5 or 95. Big, brave lads.

One last chance. A run down the wing, the cross. The keeper's lost and the dream is over as the ball is knocked home. For the Red Army, it's too much. As the Blue indulge in wild celebration, the Red move en masse. Their team, so often unable to deliver, have failed at the last. Now it is for them to gain victory. Fists and boots fly. Blood is spilt, it doesn't matter whose. Police, horses, dogs, all are now involved, before some kind of order is restored. The final whistle brings with it renewed chaos. The Blues are delirious, the Reds in rage and the players under attack. A cloud of hate covers the arena like never before. Even for this fixture, as supporters we have reached the bottom of the pit. All of us.

I look on, elated at the result, scared for my life and gloating as I watch another dagger bury itself into the back of the enemy. Television is also looking on as more fists and boots fly, so for 'them' this must surely mean the end. All the emotions at once brings my body to a high, one that is shared by the ranks of Blue that surround me. Some even try to attack back (yes, we have the brave warriors, too). Go on, lads, an eye for an eye. I know I shouldn't feel like this, for now I am as bad as they are. But, God knows, I want it.

The players have gone but the pitch continues to play host to another game. Many of the supporters have stayed on to watch the battle. Are these the supporters that want this stopped, the ones that say there is no place for this kind of thing? Is it, for them, like watching motor racing? They don't want to see anyone crash or get injured, yet the danger is exciting. Deep in the back of their mind, who really knows what they think?

Time passes and now I am scared. All that remains is Blue, but I can hear the sirens outside and see the ambulance men and women mopping up the aftermath in front of me. I don't wear Blue in this part of town, but many do and the sidestreets will be dangerous for them. Forty-five minutes pass and the gates open. We all live in this city, but no one wants to go out there. We all pass these people in the streets, but no one wants to meet up with them this particular afternoon. Mums and dads hold children close.

As I walk in silence with my friend, we look for the danger, our eyes checking every sidestreet for strangers, Reds. My legs tingle and my stomach churns as three men turn the corner and walk towards us. Heads down, we safely pass and the fear subsides. The safety of the car brings relief and the chance to reflect. Today, there had been real desire to hurt, to maim people for no more than the colour of the scarf they choose to wear. There will have been many other attacks in the surrounding streets that will go unnoticed. Was it really worth it? Was it really worth risking my life for? Oh, yes – because now I am safe, I got away with it. Next time, I may not be so lucky.

The two Bristol sides are far from being the only teams down in the west of England. Turn left at Bristol and eventually you will end up in another town with a very interesting derby game, which can produce a highly charged atmosphere and, on occasions, a great deal of violence. While Exeter are known for having a particularly volatile little group of hooligans in the Sly Crew, their opposite numbers in Torquay have rarely hit the headlines, as Al from Exeter explains:

## EXETER CITY

A couple of seasons ago, we had a New Year's Day trip to our crap rivals, Torquay United. It's always a good day out for us; loads of fun taking liberties, due to the shit firm Torquay have. It's sad to think that Torquay have got fuck all in the way of a firm, as the resort is over-populated with those horrible Scouse bastards and fucking Jocks who have made Torquay into a miniature Liverpool or Glasgow. A right shithole.

Anyway, we had planned to travel to Torquay via BR and had a tidy firm of about 70 lads who were all pissed-up from the previous evening's partying. As it was New Year, many of the lads were still in fancy dress, gorilla suits being the most popular.

We got off the train at Torre and were immediately greeted by the local plod, who were armed with video cameras watching every move we made. Now, as I live closer to Torquay than all my Exeter comrades, I know the place inside out and to slip the police net was a doddle.

As soon as we got to the town centre, we ran a few of their lot before indulging in more beer en route to the ground. Despite having several skirmishes right outside their end, we all managed to get into their place without any interrogation from plod, and it was even better to see that they had a few unknown faces in the ground wanting to have a pop at us. To our right were about 30 blokes in their late twenties, early thirties, who were obviously well up for it.

As soon as Exeter came out onto the pitch, we started to give it the big one: E-C-F-C, E-C-F-C, etc, just to let everybody in the ground know that we were there. We then got ourselves prepared for their charge, but it never came and so two of our 'gorillas' ran at them to kick things off. As soon as the Torquay scum retaliated, we let them have it from all directions. It was sheer joy to see big gaps appearing all over the place as, once again, we had turned them over on their shitty 'Popular Side' end.

Once the Old Bill took control of the situation, the Torquay boys suddenly got brave and were giving it loads of verbal behind the police line of protection. As they were doing that, we were spotting the faces that needed to be sorted after the game. One mouthy little wind-up merchant was giving us cut-throat signs. A big mistake, as he was to find out later on.

After the game, we looked all over the place for these wankers, but to no avail. As we had thought, they had bottled it again. However, as we made our trip back to the railway station via the town centre, we came across a dozen or so of their boys up a sideroad. We legged it after them and gave them a right battering in the road outside a pub. A few locals came out to have a go, but they soon realised that we were in no mood to fuck about and after a few of them were slapped around, they dived back into the pub, which we then pelted with bottles.

Once this little encounter was over, we walked into their shopping precinct and were overjoyed to see four more of the mouthy wankers hiding in a burger bar. A couple of our lads ran in and battered them, and the place ended up a right mess. Needless to say, the front window was put out, just for the crack. The police then turned up and escorted us back to the station, and then all the way back to Exeter.

It's a shame to think that we only treat Torquay as a piss-take day out and never treat it with any seriousness. Things would be very different if our real local rivals, Plymouth, were in the same division.

For those with an interest in the hooliganism issue, mention of Plymouth FC means only one thing: the Central Element. It has to be said that the two of us have a soft spot for Plymouth and their supporters for, as Eddy has already mentioned, we met a few of their lads during Euro 96 and they were top boys. Really up for a laugh. However, the fact remains that among the Central Element are a very active group of hooligans and that should not be forgotten. Proof of this, if any were needed, came when the fixture list for the 1997–98 season threw out what was for them, a local derby for their opening game. As David from Plymouth explains:

## THE CENTRAL ELEMENT

As soon as we heard it was Bristol Rovers, we knew we had to go. Although not as good as City's firm, they still have a big mob and that will do nicely for us.

Organising this one was a pain in the arse. Hours spent on the phone, going to see people, hiring minibuses and cars, etc. In the end, we had a good firm of about 60 lads including three top boys from the HYC (Huddersfield Young Casuals) who came to, shall we say, 'observe'!

Now driving through Bristol with two mini-buses and six cars full of semi-pissed up blokes isn't easy, so we decided to park a fair way from the ground so as not to be lifted by the Old Bill. Besides, the game was all-ticket and no one had any but we were there anyway, we were mobbed up and were right up for it.

As we moved towards the ground, we still hadn't seen any Old Bill and then two lads who had been on the scout for us came back and told us that Rovers had about 200 boys at the Wellington pub near the ground. At first I didn't believe them and told them to shut the fuck up as I didn't want people to start shitting it, but we decided to go up and have a look-see! We didn't see any Old Bill until we were nearly at the Wellington, and even then they were too stupid to realise who we were and what we were about to do. We stopped a short way up the road to let the others catch up, but could see the pub was mobbed inside and out. Then it all went off and I've never seen it go like it did. No hesitation on our part: straight across the road and into them. They couldn't believe it, it went mental; glasses, bottles, cans, they chucked the fucking lot at us but still we steamed in and some of their boys got it big time. We ran them right into their pub and then we stood outside giving it the big one: 'We are Central Element!' Of course, when we had been there a few minutes and they had regrouped, they charged out of the pub and at us. Fuck me, that was mental, they just kept coming.

Credit to them, they ran us back across the road, but then the cry went up to stand and everyone turned and stood firm. They were everywhere and they were really pissed at us. Then there was the usual stand off, loads of 'come on then you cunts', open palms and all that shit – fuck me, if I had a quid for every time I've seen that – while we're all stood there across the road armed up. I've got a stone the size of a fist in my hand while others have got glasses and bottles left over from the pub. Then, what looked like their top boy walks out the front and starts mouthing off at us big time. Well, we're not having any of that so he gets bombarded with all this stuff and then we ran at them. I've never seen 60 lads run so many. They shit right out and then the Old Bill came steaming in and split us up. They had obviously decided to end our fun and escort us into the ground, but the trouble was we didn't have tickets. As we stood there while the police worked out what to do next, the Rovers lads started to get brave again and began giving us more mouth, so we took the piss a bit more before the Old Bill decided that if we had no tickets, we had to fuck off out of Bristol, now!

It was only 2.45 and as we were being marched back to the buses, with the Old Bill in tow and two plain-clothed wankers with their video camera, the word went out, we were going to pay Exeter a visit.

Arriving at scum city just after their game with Chester, we decided to head for its main pub, the Vines, to see if their poor excuse for a firm were there, which, of course, they weren't. They must have known we would show, but they wouldn't have expected us until about 7.30, long after the Bristol game. But us arriving two hours early really fucked them so we sat down for a quiet drink and total piss-take in their main pub. As we were settling down, four of their main lads walked in and as they clocked us, they must have shit their pants! The landlady, seeing what was happening, told them to leave which brought howls of laughter and loads of abuse from our lot. Imagine being asked to leave your own pub! Once they got outside, they were straight on the mobiles and then they fucked off. Having taken the piss again, we decided to drink up and go and look for them. We were walking through the city centre when, at fucking last, they showed. There were about 30 of them but as we steamed towards them, 25 decided to do a Linford Christie while the other five made the brave decision to take us on. What a fucking mistake that was! After these five had been well turned over, we decided to turn our attention to the rest of the British 5000 metre sprint team and headed for the Duke of York which was one of their other pubs and where, we hoped, these wankers had run to.

As we got to the top of the road, there they were. Right outside the pub but this time they had two Old Bill with them. Within seconds, the police were on the radio and that was it for us, game over. We were on our way back to Plymouth by 7.30 and then out on the piss. But what a result! First day of the season, two different cities, two different firms and two definite results. We even had a few calls from Bristol City lads and some from Cardiff's Soul Crew who all confirmed that we had done the business.

# Chapter 9

# The Midlands

Anyone who has ever had the good fortune to live in the Midlands, as Dougie has, will know that the people there worship their football in a way unlike any other region of Britain. The passion for the game is astonishing, but more importantly, so is the good humour and the banter.

With so many teams in the region, the derby games come thick and fast. For the supporters this means frayed nerves and bitten fingernails, but for the hooligan groups it means more opportunities for violence and they relish it. Make no mistake, if you wrote down the names of the clubs with the worst-behaved followings in British football, a very large percentage of them would be from this part of the country.

The passion involved in a local derby encourages us all to make judgements on those we fondly refer to as the scum, which they would counter word for word. The supporters of Wolverhampton Wanderers and West Bromwich Albion offer a prime example. The Black Country derby involves two teams that seem forever destined to let their supporters down, making victory over one another even more important. Both clubs have a large following and suffer from having an element hell bent on causing trouble. Mr H. puts forward a Wolves point of view:

## THE HAPPY WANDERER ·

The first things all children should be taught when they are born are that the Wolves are the greatest team on earth, they play at Molineux and that it should be everyone's duty to hate West Brom. The Black Country derby has to be one of the most one-sided derbies in the country as the scum down the road have a piss-pot of an excuse for a firm that calls itself the Section 5, whatever the fuck that is. They always claim to come down here in numbers, but the truth is that they turn up about two minutes before kick-off, when every other fucker is in the ground. Then they walk through the shopping centre abusing old ladies and call that a result. Well fucking hard, that is.

At their place it's a very different story. We tell them we're coming and we turn up in numbers. A few years back, they tried to put on a show and greeted us with a bottle-throwing attack before running back into the Halfway House pub. We followed them in with CS gas and smashed the place to fuck after they did a runner through the back doors. The police filmed the whole lot and followed it up with dawn raids, but it was worth it. The lads all got off with it in the end, anyway: 2–0.

Their fans are always writing whingeing letters to the papers about the treatment they get when they come to Molineux, but they're too thick to realise that if they don't like it, don't fucking come, then, you pillocks. For us, 1991 was a good one. They were attacked at half-time with a mass of bricks and other missiles that had somehow been smuggled into the ground. We ran them all over the place before that game and they ended up back at the station asking for a police escort. Once they got it, they all started mouthing off again. What a joke. At the end of the match, the police took the intelligent decision to let all the fans leave at the same time; it was murder. As they came up the steps and across the road, we charged across the dual carriageway and into the escort.

Only about 30 of their lads had the bottle to stand their ground. At least they were prepared to take a hiding for their club, not like the rest of them. There were all sorts of people running with our firm that day, even some of the more respectable members of the supporters' club were there. Well, it *was* the scum, after all, and everyone has to do his duty.

In January '97, they did the usual late-arrival trick but this time we waited for the fuckers. They were spotted at about five to three with a fair mob of around 60, but this time they were taken completely by surprise. They thought they were the bollocks until around 150 of us turned out of the pub and ran them all over the place. A few of their lads took a right hiding; maybe they will think twice next time. You can't hide forever, lads!

So that seems fairly cut and dried – the Wolves lads maintain a historical superiority over their rivals. But writing these books has given us an insight into the way fans think, and if you took the above tale from Molineux and told it to an Albion fan, he'd probably laugh in your face before pouring your pint over your head. He'd then begin to tell you the *real* truth, as does Mr C. below. Here is *his* opinion on the none too friendly relationship between the two sets of supporters.

## *GO BAG YOURSELF A WOLF*

Wolves is short for wank. Wank fans, wank team, wank ground and a wank firm. I can't wait until 4.50pm every Saturday to hear that the shit have lost again. I love to think of all those wankers moaning about how they really should be in with the big boys, rather than the likes of Reading, Oxford, etc. Face it, losers, you're shit, second-rate. The whole shitty excuse you call a football club is second-rate, accept it.

To say the rivalry is pure evil is an understatement. Being a Baggie means having to have eyes in the back of your head when we play the scum, as they won't ever have it away face-to-face. The Wolves lads love a battle when they outnumber any other firm by about five to one, but any less than that and they are soon on their toes. You know it's true, lads, and so does every other firm in the country. You're known for it, and not much else.

After we won 2–1 down their place the other year, they tried to barricade us in and stop us getting out. Why? Not too clever, really, if what you want is to fight us. The lads were getting really angry and chairs were being ripped out and thrown all over the place. When the police finally let us out, the fun really began. Our lads headed for the subway where their main mob usually hang out, but the police had blocked it all off. Some of our lads worked their way around to the back entrance and went for it from there. With no police to hide behind, they did the off on their own patch. Total humiliation for any so-called firm. It wasn't as if there were that many of our lot there to run them, but off they went, bye! It went off all over the place after that, as they tried to get a bit of respect back, but the Albion had done what they always wanted to do: run the scum on their own doorstep. What made me laugh was that the police praised the Albion fans for their good behaviour that day.

Mark, another Baggie, adds a little more fuel to the argument.

## A BIG DAY OUT

This year, 50 or so of us met up in the local for the trip down to Molineux. For this match, tickets had gone on general sale, giving us the chance to mob up and give a little payback for the attack on the mums, dads and kids that they had carried out the year before. The scum are shit like that; they won't wait for a firm to have it off with, they'll do anyone else and think that does their reputation good. Well, it makes you look wankers, lads, not hard.

We caught a bus taking us right into the middle of the town and headed for their pub, the Varsity. The police were nowhere, so on the way we put windows through on three different pubs. We were really pumped up and wanted to do as much damage as possible so those fuckers knew we had been around. This mob wasn't lads but blokes – the average age was 30, I would have said. We could see their 'boys' in the street shitting themselves and getting on their toes, but word must have got back to the Varsity because instead of the expected attack from their lot, they had barricaded the doors to keep us out. The 'mighty' Wolves doing that, at their own pub! How embarrassing, lads. After we'd put a few windows through, the police turned up to escort us away and guess what, the Wolves all came out and gave it the big one. It's always the same – when the police turn up, you get a few lads that act like they are really going nutty. Where were you 10 minutes earlier, eh lads? I haven't laughed that much in years. When it's even numbers, everyone knows that there is only one team in the Black Country. And it isn't fucking Wolves.

As you can see, the feelings between the two groups run deep and almost mirror each other. We must state that, rightly or wrongly, the impression we get from Wolves fans is that the Albion firm are no match for their own hooligans. They look down upon them with a degree of arrogance that leads them to look further afield for a more even contest.

## STOKE UP A FIRE

All the Wolves lads really hate having to waste our time going down and proving to the scum that they are nothing, when there are far better firms in the Midlands to take on. You can't enhance your reputation by giving the Albion yet another hiding.

This area, though, has the potential for some real crackers. Over the years, we've had some great rucks with Birmingham, the Villa, Leicester, Forest, the list goes on; but the one game that 90 per cent of the time guarantees a ruck is with Stoke. They are always out in numbers. Their place is well naughty to visit and, unlike the scum, they always come down here ready to mix it.

In '94, we went to Stoke in a minibus followed by another car-load. As we entered the city, we passed a pub called the Wheatsheaf where outside were gathered a large firm of 75–100 Stoke lads, drinking and on the scout for any Wolves firm coming in by road. Things like that always get the blood racing – you may get away without a hiding there and then, but if someone follows you in a car or on a motorbike from the pub, then you're fucked for parking up because they will sort you out later. Luckily, we passed quickly and never got noticed. Once parked up, the lads decided we had enough numbers to go back and cause a bit of a row. I was shitting it, to be honest. There was only 20 of us and I thought we were certain to get slaughtered. But you can't be seen to bottle out, because you won't be invited back. Sometimes you have to take a hiding if you want to be involved, and I thought this was going to be one of those days.

We walked back up towards the pub as casually as 20 blokes can while not trying to look like a mob. The Stoke lads were having a look, wondering who the fuck we were. I've been in the same situation as they were then, you know what you're thinking: either they must be totally thick or complete nutters. Just as we started to square up, the police came flying in from nowhere. I was well relieved, to tell the truth. It's one of the few times I've been pleased to see the police at a ruck! The police led us off back down the road.

The Stoke lads came running out and dived off down a sideroad. Within a minute, they suddenly appeared right in front of us. We were well outnumbered and the

Stoke lads obviously expected us to do a runner, but we couldn't turn back because the police were behind us. Some of the lads started to run at the Stoke boys, so we all followed – fuck getting left on your own in a situation like that. What a mad couple of minutes that was, with the police chasing us and us running at the Stoke lads, who didn't have a clue what to do! Their lads at the back started throwing beer bottles and glasses, which stopped us and gave the police time to catch up and get between us. After the obligatory exchange of verbal, we were pushed off down another road as they were 'guided' back to their pub. We were more than a little pleased with ourselves at the show we had put on, and no one had even got nicked.

The police seemed happy that they had separated us, and led us to a pub where they could post a load of their lads to keep an eye on us. We got word that the main Wolves mob were at a pub called the Phoenix and so in twos and threes we left the pub we were in and, with the police supposedly keeping watch, made our way down there instead. There must have been around 100 or so Wolves in the pub, getting well pissed-up. They were well pleased after hearing about our previous meeting, as it would mean the Stoke lads would be more than up for winning back a bit of face later in the afternoon.

Word went around that we would pay the Stoke lads another visit at the Wheatsheaf and a set time was agreed to leave the pub en masse. The pub emptied and I would imagine the landlord found himself short of about 200 pint glasses, as the lads took everything from used bottles to ashtrays and pool balls to use in the raid. As we turned into the high street, we could see loads of police lined up, obviously expecting something to happen but not having an idea of where we were. It was clear that we wouldn't get back up to the Stoke lads, so we just unloaded there and then. It was mad, glass was flying everywhere. The police forced us out of the high street using dogs and horses, and the Stoke lads soon turned up, going berserk. The police had a real riot on their hands here and it went on for fucking ages, with us trying to get at the Stoke, then them having a pop at us. It just kept going backwards and forwards. The police certainly earned their overtime that day.

That was the Wolves putting on a good show that day. They knew we had been to town and so did every other fucker in that high street. Fair play to the Stoke lads, though, they would have been well ready to mix it if we could have got at each other. I often wonder if it would be better for the police to just get us into a sideroad and let us get on with it! The Stoke lads have brought good numbers to Molineux ever since then and made a good account of themselves, and we can't help but have a bit of respect for that. Unlike the Albion.

For those who indulge in violence at games, having a local rival with only a small mob must be very frustrating. Especially when your own mob is one of the most (rightly) feared in football. This seems to be the case with Stoke and Port Vale, because for Stoke's Naughty Forty, the fact that Vale never show is the source of great disappointment, as the following anecdote – anonymous by request – is only too ready to confirm:

## THE POTTERIES DERBY

Port Vale have never done Stoke and they never will. That's a simple fact. What mob they have got is so small, it's hardly worth bothering about. You'd think that by now we'd be so used to that that we wouldn't give a shit about them, but you'd be wrong. Mere mention of those wankers sends us into a rage, because they never show. Not against us, nor any other decent mob, and that's pathetic. For years, we've tried to set it up with them and they come up with the same old shit about where they'll be and when they will be there, but they've never shown. They've got no bottle at that club and, worse than that, no pride.

We thought we'd finally sorted it with them for last season. For the last derby at our beloved Victoria Ground, Vale needed a win to have a chance of promotion and that was something we couldn't have. I mean, could you imagine remembering the last derby game as a win and promotion for your local rivals? No way.

With so much at stake, we knew that this time they had to come – and we heard on the Wednesday before the game that, for once, they were definitely showing. Not only that, but word was out that they were planning to demolish the Naughty Forty once and for all, and there was no way we could put up with talk like that.

The game was on a Sunday – because of the television, probably – and on the day, we all met up at one of our locals quite early. Much to our delight, the place was filling up pretty quickly and as well as the usual lads, a good few old faces were in there as well. Just to round things off, about 20 of the mental Fenton lads and some Dundee casuals came into the pub to boost the numbers up even further.

By about two o'clock, with the pub rammed full of mental boys, we started to get a bit anxious. The coppers were all over the place and if they sussed us or got hold of the Vale tossers, then nothing would happen. But then it did.

One of our lads came running into the boozer saying that there were about 50 Vale lads walking in our direction with no police escort at all. This was music to our ears and seconds later, we heard their singing. We looked out of the window and there they were, walking down the road towards us and mouthing off at a few Stoke fans. In all my life, I don't think I'll ever see a pub empty as fast as that again. We all steamed out and just laid into the cunts. As we battered them, they scattered but there were so many of us, they didn't have a chance. And when the coppers finally arrived, we just went back into the pub to watch the arsewipes limp off to the ground with their escort. Excellent.

Inside the ground, the atmosphere was electric and I'm sure that if Vale had won that day, then the stadium would have been wrecked. As it was, Stoke won 2–0 and we just sang and celebrated throughout. Not just for the win, but because we'd ruined their chances of promotion. After all, can it get any better than that?

At the end of the game, we made our way round to the Vale end but the tossers had already pissed off, leaving around 400–500 lads very disappointed. We went back to the boozer well pleased with our day's work and settled in for the night, when someone suggested we go to Vale after the bastards. Next thing I knew, we were outside stopping taxis, or grabbing any other form of transport we could, to get over to their end of town.

Inevitably, the coppers caught some of the lads on their way over, but we still managed to get a mob of around 150 lads together and as soon as we arrived, we made our way to the best-known Vale drinking hole. Before we knew what was happening, their lads were piling out of the pub and running at us with glasses and bottles. There were only two coppers around and so we forgot about them and steamed down the road to meet the Vale head-on. Predictably, they turned and ran, but we caught a load of them and really let them have it. After that, we just went on the rampage as a show of force and to let all the wankers know that Stoke will always have the superior lads in Stoke-on-Trent.

We did them twice in one day, once outside their own pub, and left a trail of destruction in our wake. Not only that, but we stopped them getting promotion. Magic.

Derby County and Nottingham Forest are two teams that find themselves going up and down like a pair of whore's drawers.

Their rivalry may not mean much to us, but W. M. seems to think it's quite important:

## IT'S NOT COUNTY WE HATE, IT'S COUNTY

Derby County, two words always guaranteed to make any Forest fan laugh. The team that can boast of having the supporters with the lowest IQs in the country and possibly the world. Doh! The best thing to come out of Derby is the A52 straight back to Nottingham.

You see, Derby have always had these bizarre delusions of grandeur, dating from way back when, which continually make them the laughing stock of the East Midlands. I mean, even Leicester Shitty have won something now; catch up, lads. They love to bleat on about Cloughie, saying that Forest wouldn't have won the League or the European Cup (twice) – I'll repeat, the League or the European Cup (twice) – if it hadn't been for him. What the hell does that mean? So he saw the fucking light then, didn't he, you sheep-shaggers.

At last, it appears that even they have realised that the flea-pit they had for a ground was not the 'atmospheric little place' that they were so fond of, but a complete shithole that needed pulling down. Their constant claim for being the most loyal fans in the country is a total joke. Loyal doesn't mean following an inept bunch of no-hopers for years on end, only to wake up one day and realise that you should have been watching that successful team in red and white from down the road all those years instead. No, that's not loyalty, that's called being a wanker all your life.

Oh, how we loved watching the sheep get beat in the play-off the other year. I never thought I would want Leicester to win a game of football, but when Paul Williams ducked out of the way and so let that goal in, I shit my pants with joy. It made our automatic promotion that year – helped by a 2–0 win at their place, may I add

– all the more sweet. Thank you, Derby County, you do make us laugh.

Actually, I suppose we should be like every other city with two teams and hate our neighbours, Notts County, but what's the point? Mansfield can do that.

An alternative view of this rivalry was hard to find, until this little note fell into our postbox one day. It was signed 'Roger T. Ram' and although the language is a bit basic, we think he gets his message across pretty well.

## FOREST?

Forest? Oh yeah, I remember, that lower division side supported by cunts.

We all know only too well that when the derby fixture gets underway, all current form goes out of the window. The fact that your team are 15 points adrift at the bottom of the league and the scum are 10 points clear at the top means nothing. If you are wearing your lucky pants and have caught the same bus, at the same time, followed the ritual of going to the same chip shop and managed to win again on the fruit machine, then you know that you are in with a chance. If, however, you have not yet worked out the right combination of superstitions that will guarantee victory, then you can always pray that the great goddess Banana Skin will place herself under the feet of the enemy.

The following account comes from R.M. (The Penguin) and expresses the sheer joy we have all felt at some stage when getting one over on our rivals. Oh, how I can see John Barnes rising now to head in that extra-time winner in the FA Cup at Vicarage Road. 'We beat the scum 4–3' . . . 'Wembley, Wember-ley' . . . etc.

## BOXING DAY 1982

As a kid growing up, Blues versus Villa days were something both to enjoy and dread at the same time. Our area Light Hall was strictly 50–50; if your team lost, you were reminded about it every day at every breaktime.

This day I feared more than any other. Blues were bottom of the old First Division with only three wins all season, while Villa were on a high, having claimed the ultimate club prize in Europe, the European Cup, just seven months earlier.

There was something different about this particular match from the start. Not only was it Christmas – which always adds to the atmosphere, as family and friends you wouldn't usually see are also in there – but it was Ron Saunders's first real Blues–Villa derby since walking out of Villa Park nine months previous, just as Villa were on the verge of their greatest achievement ever. No one doubted that it was Ron's team that had won that trophy, and the Villa fans were both amazed and still seething at his departure. The fact that he had moved across the city to the Blues just rubbed salt into the wounds.

'You must be fucking mad, Saunders, Saunders,' sang the Villa fans, and to be honest, I think that most Bluenoses agreed. At St Andrews, Saunders had inherited a team of limited ability, and with no money to spend, he had to dive into the lower end of the transfer market to look for bargain players. He had even had the nerve to go back to Villa and snatch Noel Blake and Robert Hopkins from under their noses. Both players were promised first-team football at Birmingham and this fixture clearly gave them the opportunity to prove a few points to the Villa management.

This particular game also took place during what was the worst period for football violence in this country and all the usual tensions that surround the derby match had risen. I remember the day of the game vividly. First, catching the packed 92 bus from the Stratford Road, Shirley, with a group of school mates singing our heads off, before arriving at Camp Hill roundabout and walking up the hill to the ground with my stomach in knots. As we got closer to the ground, the atmosphere became more hostile, more volatile and more incredible. There were thousands swarming around the ground. Everywhere you turned, people, police, horses, dogs. There were meat wagons, people singing and shouting. St Andrews was like a cauldron ready to boil over at any moment. The place was electric and I wouldn't have missed it for the world.

The Villa fans were headed off towards the Tilton End as we made our way onto the Kop. Somehow we made our way towards the middle, losing two friends on the way. You couldn't move for love nor money, come kick-off; how they got them all in, I'll never know. In front and to our left was a sea of Blue, to the right only Claret. A huge roar greeted the gladiators onto the pitch, as the two sets of fans vocally battled for supremacy. 'Keep Right On' from the Blues, 'Villa, Villa' from the Clarets. Boring bastards.

The tension had clearly got to the players and after five minutes came one of those heart-stopping moments we all fear. Gary Shaw broke through the Blues defence and chipped the advancing Tony Coton (*who later moved onto much better things at Watford – sorry, we had to add that bit*). As the crowd drew its breath, Mark Dennis rushed back and somehow chested the ball down on the goal-line. Any sane person would then have hoofed that ball over the top of the main stand at that stage, but our Mark decided to exchange a couple of passes with Kevin Dillon inside the six-yard box as the Villa front line moved in for the kill. Thirty thousand people shouting 'Clear the fucking thing!' finally registered inside his brain and the danger was over. If we had known then that Villa wouldn't have another chance in the whole game, my heart might have handled the situation a little better.

Blues started to play with more confidence, moving forward and putting the Villa defence on the back foot. Then came the moment most players can only dream of. Noel Blake had been greeted with taunts from the Villa fans whenever he got near the ball: 'Villa reject, Villa reject,' being screamed at him by 8,000 people. A long cross was put into the Villa penalty area. Mick Ferguson rose at the back and headed it down into the path of the advancing Blake, whose first-time sidefoot shot crashed into the roof of the net. Before the ball had hit the floor, a roar went up that must have nearly lifted the roof off the Kop. They must have heard that over at The Hawthorns. The Tilton fell silent.

Villa were rattled as Blues dominated the rest of the half. Two players in particular had the games of their lives that day, Kevin Dillon and Ian Handysides, and that against what was 'theoretically' the best club side in Europe!

If the first half was delicious, then the second was caviar. Blues were completely running the show. The one and only time Villa broke, that most hated of all Villa players, Gary Shaw, missed in quite spectacular fashion, much to our delight, as we always thought him over-rated and arrogant. This led to hoots of derision from the Blues faithful, ending with a chorus of the highly original, 'Who the Shaw is Gary fuck?'

The second goal was sure to come and, on the hour-mark, it did. Curbishley hit a beautiful defence-splitting pass for Handysides to run onto. As Rimmer – an unfortunate name for anyone, let alone a Villa player – came charging out from his goal, Mr H. calmly slid the ball under his body and into the back of the net. If there was ever a time to register your first goal for a team, then it couldn't be better than in the derby fixture. It ensured god-like status for eternity. The Kop was in pandemonium. That very moment was the time I personally learnt never to stand against a crowd barrier, as I had the air knocked out of me following the crowd-drop from behind. Luckily, the crowd kept me on my feet, but in those days it would have been easy for someone to have been crushed, like the poor fans at Hillsborough were. No one would have noticed until it was too late.

By now, the game was effectively over. Villa were desperate, kicking the ball anywhere as they tried to resist the onslaught of a rampaging Blues side. With 10 minutes to go, Rimmer failed to hold onto a shot and Ferguson tapped in the third, as the rows and rows of Villa dejectedly looked on in disbelief. Ferguson very nearly added a fourth in the final minute, but that would have just been greedy. Villa had been hammered. The final whistle brought a standing ovation with cheering and singing like I had never heard before. The Villa ran off quicker than they had run all day, without even turning to applaud their own fans, many of whom had made their excuses and left anyway.

It is hard to remember ever being so happy. Three–nil against the European champions, who just happened to be the Villa. Did I dream it all? I don't think so. Merry Christmas, everybody!

As a postscript to the above, we picked up on one piece of information guaranteed to cheer up any Villa fan reading this. The very next season, Mick Ferguson, the scorer of the third goal that day, was loaned out to Coventry City. Birmingham were just about holding their own that season until a particularly nasty home Cup defeat drained the confidence of the supporters and players. The club slid dangerously towards the relegation zone and on the final day found themselves needing to beat Southampton at St Andrews in order to stay up. They only managed a 0–0 draw. But at that point, all was not lost because if Coventry City failed to win, then the Blues would still survive. Unfortunately, the Sky Blues did manage to get the victory they needed and Birmingham were relegated. Guess who scored Coventry's winner? One Mick Ferguson, on loan from Birmingham City!

Oh, and by the way: just in case you wanted to know, that Cup defeat that had such an effect on the club was an FA Cup quarter-final loss at St Andrews – City 1, Watford 3. Incidentally, Watford had beaten L*t*n 4–3 in a replay previously, before going onto Wembley. Sorry, did we mention that earlier? Oh, the twisty, turny life of a football fan!

# PART FIVE
# North

# Chapter 10
# It's Grim Up North

Those of us fortunate enough to live in the south of our glorious country know only too well that the north is good for only one thing: it provides a buffer zone between us and Scotland.

In the case of football fandom, the north provides ample excuse to travel with our clubs and experience that joy of returning south after our team has, hopefully, done the job it was supposed to. We also get to experience such culinary delights (?) as meat and potato pies and mushy peas, although to be fair, the best chips are always found up north. But we are not here to sing the praises of north or south, just to talk about the local rivalries that exist within the game. In the case of the north of England, they are many and are all too often ferocious affairs.

For this book, we expected a great deal of material from both Manchester and Sheffield but, despite our best efforts, received very little. The reason for that escapes us, because the Sheffield clubs are certainly among the most passionate rivals in Britain.

Clearly, every soccer thug relishes the prospect of a local derby game, both on and off the field. The fact that the fans at the other end of the ground live in the next town, the next street, or even the next bedroom, gives the whole day added significance. In the north east, when the 'big three' meet, the

161

possibilities for violence are very real. Indeed, as J. H., a Newcastle fan from North Tyneside, relates, the clubs don't even have to meet on the pitch for the fans to indulge:

## THE GEORDIES

One weekend, we thought we'd treat ourselves to a good day out and have a pop at the scum (Sunderland), who we hate with a passion. On the Saturday in question, we were due to play Middlesbrough away and although many think that this is a local derby, they're over 40 minutes down the A19 and as far as we're concerned, it's just another game. The Boro had been getting a good name for themselves over the years, although they've never created much when they're on our patch. Lately, though, they'd resorted to giving our lads grief in and around the local nightclub circuit, so it was about time they were taught a lesson by the top boys in the north east.

All the old faces were contacted – including a few who had settled down and had been well out of it for a good while – and on the day, we had an evil mob of around 100 milling around 'the Shrine' of Newcastle Central station by about nine o'clock. However, this wasn't all down to the attraction of a day out at Boro. We were also going to pay the scum a surprise visit, as the Mackems were playing at home.

Everything was organised to escape the police clamp-down, because we knew that once they got hold of us, that would be it. So we bought the train tickets and went past Boro to Darlington. Once there, one of the lads had organised a pub owner to open his bar for us at about 10. So there we were, having a few sherbets and getting into the mood.

One o'clock came and we all set off to the station. The two carriages we took over were rammed full of lads 'up for it', and not one runner among us. Anyhow, talk about coppers being thick as pigshit, for when we pulled into Boro's station, the platform and entrance was full of plods looking menacing . . . but we were coming from the other direction, so our platform was empty! We seized the chance and the carriages emptied within seconds. It was five to two and we knew Boro would be in or around the two pubs situated within yards of the station. Everyone was at the pace of a quick walk on the unmanned platform, and we made it out of the station just as the police finally realised what was happening and they were screaming at us to stop. Some chance!

All our eyes were focused on the first pub as our relatively quiet mob steamed across the road. Outside the pub there were a couple of their smart lads, who looked at us in sheer terror. They lobbed their pints at us, but it was too late. We were on top of them, fighting to get through the pub entrance. Tunnel vision took over as the Boro were getting whacked left, right and centre, but all the surroundings were a blur. The sound of windows breaking, shouting and screaming, not to mention approaching police sirens, only heightened the buzz. Someone had let off some CS gas, which must have been one of them as we weren't tooled up at all, and suddenly the police were in the middle of it all. At that point, we pulled out and as the police were stuck in the pub, we steamed down to the next pub, which was about 100 yards away.

We must have looked like a swarm of wasps going down that road. By this time, some of their lads, about 20, had come out of the pub and were giving us the come-on, but we were all on a roll and just ran into them, fists and boots flying. There were a number of lads sparked out completely and a couple huddled up in a ball just trying to get out of it, but once again the police were soon in the middle of it and we pulled out. Due to our numbers, we were now in control of our own movements and we gathered at the corner of a crossroads to regroup.

Still no one was around to have a pop at us, probably because they didn't have a clue what the fuck was going on and they were shitting it. By the time we decided to move, the coppers were all over the place with horses and dogs, so we moved off into a housing estate and began moving through the back lanes. With everyone still on a giant high, we saw a massive mob of their lot, about 150 lads, and they were angry as fuck. Before they could see us, we just went at them as fast as we could. Before we could get there, though, three riot vans appeared and drove straight in front of us. They almost ran down some of our faster runners, but they stopped us going forward and then another couple of vans pulled in behind us. The bastards had us trapped in a little back lane, while the Boro lads were lobbing stuff at us over the top of them before the coppers moved them on. Realising that the police meant business, myself and four others (including two members of Shrewsbury's English Border Firm who had been invited along for the day, a friendship that had been formed during Italia 90 after we'd been locked up for the night together) decided to leg it between the vans, the main reason being that one of the lads couldn't risk another court appearance.

Walking around an area you don't know so well is bad enough, but when the locals are hellbent on killing you, you could say the five of us were well on the edge! It was too risky going to the game and far too dangerous to risk going back to the station for a while, so we had a few pints in a shitty little pub until after kick-off.

When we arrived back in Newcastle, we were astonished to find all our lot on the other fucking platform. The Boro coppers had decided that the only way to deal with such a big mob was to get it out of town, and fast. So they had just searched them all, took a few videos and then put them on an express train back to the 'Toon'! The five of us would have been better off 'supposedly' getting lifted! Once the dozy coppers had escorted them back to Newcastle and fucked off, our lads had just crossed the platform and were waiting for the next train to Sunderland.

Apparently, the scum weren't expecting us until after their home game, about six o'clock, the chosen venue being the Windmill pub. Fuck Queensberry rules, we decided to use the element of surprise again and turned up at about 4.30. But as we walked out of the station, it was clear that their pub was still full of lads, and a couple of scouts soon sussed us. As we took off towards them, they came pouring out of the pub and we met head-on on some waste ground. As usual, they were flapping around like headless chickens, totally unorganised and shitting themselves, and we stood our ground for a good few minutes. We certainly had the upper hand, anyway – not just because of the fact that we had already been at it and were full of confidence, but because we're full of hatred for them. The coppers then came screaming in and unfortunately, some of our lads were arrested as our soft, sad rivals did a runner.

The ones who made it home certainly had a good drink that night in the Bigg Market, and the whole day's events are talked about on a regular basis. In the space of a few hours, we humiliated our two closest 'opponents' and proved that they're nowhere near being in the same league as the Geordies.

With both Sunderland and Middlesbrough being relegated from the Premier League at the end of the 1996–97 season the re-emergence of the clubs' traditional rivalry was inevitable, given their disappointment. However, the 1997–98 season saw the activities of the supporters plunge to new depths and there is simply no excuse for some of the things that have gone on between these two sets of fans. The fact that both sets of supporters attempt to justify their actions in any way makes it all the more astonishing. An example of this was sent to us by Mike, who describes himself as 'a Boro boy through and through'. He sent us his account of what was a particularly nasty and dangerous incident that could have had fatal consequences.

## THE A66

Now there's never been any love lost between the Boro and Sunderland. Just like any derby game there's always a little trouble but this season has seen more than most and has ensured that, from now on, there's going to be more and more. Here's how it all started.

We – the Boro – travelled to the Stadium of Shite early in the season fully expecting a bit of bother because we had kicked the shit out of their lot down at our place the year before. But the scenes we were faced with were very unexpected. We won the game 2–1, but a good 10 minutes before the end we could see their lads leaving the ground. We were bracing ourselves for a bit of a ruck, but what followed was a full-scale riot.

The police were shite and seemed virtually non-exist-ent as their 'lads' were kicking the shit out of our shirts, which is fucking out of order. I personally saw an OAP get smashed in the face and loads of our lasses being spat on! We went for it with any of their lot that had the bottle to fight real men, but it didn't last long as eventually the bobbies got their act together. However, they smashed our coaches up, full of families, and even had the cheek to throw bottles and pint glasses at our disabled supporters bus as it passed a pub. Even Chelsea or Millwall at their worst wouldn't have resorted to that. Anyway, because of this incident, they were sure to receive a warm welcome the next time they came down here. So imagine our delight when we drew them in the Coca-Cola Cup, at home!

We didn't even bother to organise our lads because we were sure that revenge was on everyone's minds due to the fact that their attack on our disabled bus had been widely reported in the local press. Come the night of the match, we were looking for anyone and anything wearing stripes: women, children, old fogies, it didn't matter. We wanted to send a message out loud and clear that no cunt fucks the Boro about, let alone the fucking Mackems! All the old boys were out, the original frontline and, boy, were they up for it. I even saw one of my old teachers and my ex-driving instructor!

We heard of a few confrontations before the game but didn't witness anything ourselves. We were concentrating on after the match and didn't fancy getting locked up for slapping some shirt when the chance to do the poxy Seaburn Casuals was out there. We all agreed to congregate outside the away end 10 minutes before the final whistle, but the pigs beat us to it and, when we got there, they had a line of horses between us and the back of the stand. This allowed us to hunt around for missiles (not very difficult given that the Riverside is sited on a huge wasteland) and we were tooled up with all-sorts: bricks, broken bottles, planks of wood, the lot. We were just waiting for them to show, shouting their mouths off behind a line of police just like they always do. Anyway, they came out and just as planned, gave it the biggie. 'Come on Boro' and 'Soft as shite' rang out from the daft cunts before we shut them up with a shower of gifts. This didn't impress the police, but they couldn't hang on to any of our lot long enough to get the cuffs on as we just barged them out of the way.

By now, our mob was about 400 strong but because we were all together and the exit from the Riverside is only one long road, the bobbies soon got hold of us and it was easy for them to move us along even if it was like a death march. It took them 30 minutes to move our lot 10 yards but eventually, when a load of extra police and dogs arrived, they managed to get us away from their coaches and off up the road.

Around 50 of us eventually decided to split up and

meet again at the A66 roundabout to try and meet up with their coaches. We managed to brick a few minibuses, but no cunt dared stop and get out, and one bastard even had the cheek to drive his P-reg XR3i past with four passengers all wearing those fucking stripes we all hate. Poor bastard, he took some punishment! It was paradise: no police, because they were in town searching for us, and an endless supply of ammunition as we were running into the road to retrieve the bricks we were using!

We'd been there a good 15 minutes when we realised that God himself is a Boro fan. What did we see approaching us with no escort? Only the fucking Sunderland team coach! We showered it with every-fucking-thing in sight and when the windscreen went in, the driver's face was a picture. There's nothing you can do when your vehicle's getting smashed up by the opposition fans; if you get out you get done and if you drive through, the coach gets fucked up. So all you can do is put your foot down and hope. Thinking back, it's a wonder he didn't crash because he was watching us not the road!

Most of us saw this as the funniest thing we had ever seen in our lives, but it was also revenge for the attack on the disabled lads (and lasses). If nothing else, it makes it certain that this is one rivalry that is going to get more and more serious.

Yorkshire can be a dangerous place to visit for any football fan. It goes without saying that the Leeds hooligans are in a different league to anything else the area has to offer, mainly due to their greater numbers, but there is plenty of additional activity taking place, as certain elements of support from Bradford, Barnsley and Huddersfield battle it out. It is a part of the country that, like London, could fill a book of its own.

One of the more dangerous aspects of life among the football fans of Yorkshire is the apparently increasing use of weapons, a subject of great concern to us personally. From things we have heard over the years, we would go so far as to say that in parts of that region, we believe it is almost out of control. The following story shall remain anonymous and tells of the revenge one Bradford fan craves, following the loss of a friend.

## TROUBLE IN THE PEOPLE'S REPUBLIC

There was a time when I would go to all the matches, week after week, but not now. The derby games with Leeds, the two Sheffield clubs and Barnsley were never to be missed, but Huddersfield were the team I really hated. As I said, I don't go anymore. I don't trust myself, because the passion with which I hate them hurts so much that I could really go over the top. The reason for this? One day, one of my best friends was stabbed to death by two Town fans who jumped him. He was just 18. Can you imagine how much I hate them for that? All he was doing was walking around the shithole in his shirt.

The matches between these two have always produced their fair share of problems. One of the most talked-about occasions took place in 1994, when fans involved with Bradford's firm the Ointment attacked a known Huddersfield pub. The whole attack was filmed by an undercover police unit and the evidence was used to sentence 15 fans to a total of over 20 years in jail. All the Huddersfield fans involved claimed they were the victims of an unprovoked attack and were acting in self-defence; all escaped punishment. The question as to the excellent timing of the undercover police unit that 'just happened to be passing' has never been answered. What should be remembered is that some innocent fans could have avoided injury if the police had acted to prevent such an outbreak of violence, rather than sit safely back and film it!

Following this incident, trouble between the two showed no signs of calming down as despite the prison sentences dealt out by the courts, both firms continued to turn out in numbers. G. gives an account that proves that the police, with a little pre-planning, can actually get it right.

## *WE DON'T NEED NO OINTMENT*

The police and the clubs had been appealing for calm for weeks in the build-up to this match. They knew that both sets of fans were out to prove just who were top lads, and all the appeals in the world would never stop that from happening. Some lads from the Huddersfield Young Casuals (HYC) had been in contact with their opposite numbers in the Ointment, so we knew they were coming in numbers and they knew we were ready and waiting. The police swamped the area. They must have some good intelligence up here, as they were all over their lads when they arrived and got them straight to the ground without anything going off. Fair play to Bradford, they had brought a tidy firm and on seeing that, we knew that at some stage it would go off.

As the game started, Town were getting slaughtered. The team were 3–0 down before you knew what was happening and the City fans were really winding us up and taking the piss. Word went out for our mob to leave, even though it was still only the first half. A fair few had already made their way up the steps when Town pulled one back. The police were all over the place – they realised that something was about to happen, but didn't have a clue what. Some of the lads still wanted to make a move, and were having a go at the others to leave, when Town scored again. Now it was 3–2, there was no way anyone would leave now. Just after the start of the second half, we equalised. Their shit fans shut right up. Midway through the half, some Town fans outside fired two rockets over the stand and onto the pitch. We could see the red tracers coming over, but the players didn't and the rockets just missed them.

One of the City players started to act up that he had been hit. What a cunt. That could have cost the club thousands, as well as starting a riot in the crowd. The Town fans gave him shit and amazingly, he made a sudden recovery and came charging over, giving us the big one and shouting at us to fuck off. Players think they are so fucking hard, they make me die. I would just love to see one of them front any lad from a firm and see what would happen. They wouldn't last five seconds.

The game finally ended 3–3 and now the fun was about to start. I swear I have never seen so many police at Huddersfield. We mobbed up outside, but the police tried to keep us moving and get us away so they could let the City fans out. It was getting really heavy and the police were filming everyone, so we moved off and broke up into small groups, making it difficult for the police to keep an eye on all of us. The Bradford fans were let out and their lads tried to force their way free of the police escort, but they were all over them.

The only people to get turned over were those that travelled by car. Our lads wouldn't usually target these fans, but for a derby match any scum are fair game. Make no mistake, the two firms will have their meeting another day. The police can't keep us apart forever.

While the police got it right in the above account, they can also get it wrong – and this they did on a monumental scale in 1996, in the full glare of the television cameras. The game concerned was between Bradford City and Hull City, both clubs with a very volatile following. What follows is an examination of the Hull City fans as well as a look at the events of that fateful day. It is based on information supplied anonymously.

## TO HULL AND BACK

For many supporters viewing from a distance, the obvious derby fixture for Hull City would be Grimsby Town. However, if you look at a map, it shows that the club are actually sitting out on their own and have various derby fixtures to choose from. Indeed, the recent fortunes of the club have seen the games against Grimsby drifting off into the distant past, leaving the matches with clubs such as Scunthorpe, Doncaster and Scarborough as the main focus for local rivalry.

As the club fell down the league table, the average home attendance inevitably fell with it. Unfortunately, in a pattern repeated at numerous other clubs over the years, the hooligan element that follows the club has not fallen away in such great numbers and, as a result, now forms a greater proportion of the club's support. Here, the old chestnut that those who cause trouble are not 'real' supporters is clearly shown to be untrue. Like them or loathe them, these are the very people who form the hard core of the club's support, and they continue to follow their side through what are obviously hard times. Those who do not bother to go – or, worse, go somewhere else – would do well to remember that, because it is a fact that is all too often overlooked.

During the relegation season of 1995–96, even the police admitted that the hard core of hooligans at Hull City could reach up to 200 once trouble flared up. Trouble started early that season, as the Hull firm known as the Hull City Psychos (HCP) caused problems at their first home and away fixtures with rivals from Swindon and Rotherham. The two Coca-Cola Cup matches against Coventry City also saw major problems. In the first leg at Highfield Road, the HCP tried to steam the home end following the final whistle. The police managed to keep them at bay before the firm rampaged through the adjoining streets, damaging cars and smashing windows. For the return leg at Boothferry Park, hooligans from both clubs turned out in great numbers. To keep the two groups apart, the police were forced into mounting a large-scale operation that cost thousands of pounds.

Once again, the HCP went on the rampage through the streets prior to the derby fixture at York City on 16 December. The trouble continued during the match, as police dogs were used in order to halt a pitch invasion by the Hull hooligan contingent. Fighting also broke out in the seated areas as rival fans clashed. However, not all the trouble associated with the club at that time was the result of hooligan behaviour. A number of demonstrations took place as anger grew among the fans towards those that were running the club.

The next serious incident didn't occur until the final away game, at Peterborough United's London Road stadium. The team had struggled all season and relegation beckoned. The hooligans, looking to go out with a bang, caused problems before, during and after the match and it was here that plans were laid for the final fixture, at home to promotion candidates and serious hooligan rivals Bradford City. Indeed, it is the HCP rivalry with the Bradford firm the Ointment which leads many Hull fans to look upon Bradford as one of Hull City's biggest 'local' rivals.

The Hull city police had decided to hand over the home end of the stadium to the Bradford City supporters, much to the annoyance of the home fans. The logic behind such a decision was based on the fact that Bradford, who were playing for promotion, would bring more fans with them than there would be Hull fans attending on the day. Although this did in fact prove to be the case, such a decision was always likely to lead to only one thing on the day: serious crowd trouble.

Intelligence gathered by police spotters at the Peterborough match gave them prior warning as to the intention of the Hull hooligans to 'take back' their traditional home end and confront the Ointment on the pitch, so perhaps they might have reconsidered their original decision.

On the day, the build-up of Hull hooligans began at around 11.30am and by 12.30, the police estimated that a hard core of approximately 100 hooligans had gathered together in order to 'welcome' the Bradford fans arriving on the 12.37 train. But the first incident of the day took place on Anlaby Road nearly an hour later. As the two groups fought, police with horses were called and forced the fans apart. The Hull fans moved off towards the ground, calling in all the pubs en route to gain greater numbers. By the time the mob had reached the Griffin pub, their number had grown to 150 and fighting broke out once more as they tried to gain entry to the bar. Once again the police moved in, but by this time the mob had become highly charged and vocal. The police escorted the mob towards the stadium, as they clearly announced their intention that the place to be, for all those looking for trouble, was the South Stand. Once the group had reached the car park, they split in all directions with the intention of getting onto North Road, where the majority of the Bradford fans were congregated. The police, using dogs and horses, managed to contain the large majority, but small fights broke out as the atmosphere grew more hostile by the minute.

A large group had now decided that the best avenue to the Bradford fans would be to enter the ground and charge across the pitch! As the police continued to contain the situation outside, it was left to the club stewards to keep the peace inside the stadium. Police expected that club stewards would be responsible for all safety matters within the ground, as well as the control of the turnstiles and searching of selected supporters. This decision turned out to be an error of judgement and placed members of the public in a highly dangerous situation. The police had also gathered intelligence that the Hull hooligans had intended to continue making trouble in the ground. If they hoped that they had defused the situation outside, they were proved wrong, as the stewards were unable to cope.

Ten minutes before kick-off, the Hull hooligans who had gathered in the north-east corner invaded the pitch. The stewards offered little resistance, which is hardly surprising considering that many of them had taken on the job expecting to help people enjoy their day, rather than face a volatile mob intent on causing trouble. The Bradford fans retaliated by invading the pitch themselves and fighting broke out. Police on horseback were called in from outside and quickly cleared the pitch. Due to this action, the match was able to kick-off on time. But the mood for the afternoon had been set.

The match got underway and Hull City soon took the lead, but as the home fans were still celebrating, Bradford equalised. On seeing their team score, some Bradford fans ran onto the pitch, an action that prompted the Hull hooligans to do the same, sparking off one of the worst incidents of the day. The game was held up for 11 minutes as the police tried to keep the fighting groups apart. At the same time, the police set a ring of officers around both sets of goalposts, so that they could not be damaged. If they had been broken, then the game would have to have been abandoned. This was a particularly good move by the police, as they would certainly have faced increased problems for any rescheduled match. The match finally got restarted once the police had cleared the pitch and placed a large presence around the perimeter of the playing area, an action that, had they taken it originally, might have helped avoid the situation occurring in the first place.

Fighting continued throughout the game as the Hull hooligans on the North Terrace tried in vain to gain the upper hand. With 15 minutes remaining, a police support unit were ordered to kit themselves out in full riot gear, as it was feared that a Hull defeat would spark a further invasion of the pitch. The match finished with Bradford winning, much to the delight of the travelling fans, who left the stadium without causing further problems for the police. The Hull hooligans were clearly not happy and looking for more confrontation with their rivals. The mob regrouped and on seeing such a large police presence inside the stadium, they left to attack the Bradford fans outside.

The two groups clashed at the crossroads of Boothferry and North Road. Bricks were thrown as the Hull fans led the charge in some of the most frightening scenes ever witnessed at a Hull City match. The Bradford hooligans certainly played their part in the violence, but many families and children were caught up in the battle. The police officers in charge had made a mistake in allowing both sets of supporters out at about the same time, and the subsequent fighting lasted for some 20 minutes before police on horseback forced the groups apart. Indeed, it was made known to those in charge by the officers in the front line that if it had not been for the excellence and bravery of the police on horseback, then the situation would have been lost.

The details for the match are as follows: the home fans totalled just under 3,700, whereas there were almost 5,300 Bradford supporters present; despite the level of violence seen at the match, only six arrests were made inside the ground, with a further 11 arrested outside. The officers in charge of the policing of this match would appear to have got it badly wrong in this instance, with innocent supporters and stewards suffering as well as their own officers. Fortunately video footage of the trouble was extensive and helped identify many of those involved.

However, of more importance is the fact that there are a number of lessons to be gained from this game, and we can only hope that those in charge actually bother to learn them. The key one is that prevention is better than cure. It is also better than containment, reaction or evidence-gathering for expensive court cases, many of which will never even happen. The police had already made the game a Category C (almost guaranteed trouble) fixture as a result of the intelligence gathered at previous games, but if they knew so much, why could they not gauge the feeling among the home supporters and give them back their traditional end, and keep the Bradford fans in for a while? It may be simple with hindsight, but isn't the purpose of intelligence gathering to give you foresight?

The one saving grace for the police was that the video footage that came out of the violence caught many 'known' faces in the act and led to numerous arrests and convictions.

Barnsley are another Yorkshire club who have built a reputation for trouble, and derby games involving them can be very dodgy affairs. G. also told us how problems between the HYC and Barnsley's Five-O have escalated:

## THE FIVE-O

The Barnsley lads had been busy trying to build their reputation, and to be fair, they were doing the business and getting a good firm of around 40 lads together. They had been spouting off to some of our lads about Huddersfield and coming down to give us a lesson, so we were expecting to wait until we next played them. They had a different plan and paid a visit to town following an FA Cup game at Oldham. They walked through town singing, 'Barns-ley, Barns-ley,' and stopped off at various pubs, fighting with the locals. Word soon got around town and the Huddersfield lads started to mob up. We had a couple of lads following their movements who came back and told us that they had finally pulled up and stayed in one pub.

We mobbed up and steamed down the road and straight in at them. There was no fucking about because if the police had arrived, we wouldn't have been able to have it away and they would have claimed a complete victory. We couldn't allow them to say that they had come to town and taken the piss. The pub got blitzed. Tables, glasses, everything went through the air. The fighting moved out into the street, where two Barnsley lads had their faces slashed.

When we played them in the League Cup a few years

later, they came down in greater numbers. They were mad for a result, following that pub fight, and their firm had certainly grown in reputation. This time, they had come armed with CS gas and were attacking Town fans as they made their way to the ground. During the game, the police had things under control and the fans were behaving themselves. Then, with 20 minutes to go, all the Barnsley lads got to their feet as if they were about to leave. They obviously had pre-planned something and someone was calling the shots. The Town fans stood up as well. Then came another gas attack from the Barnsley end. The place went mental, as it mostly affected kids and families. Following the game, we were desperate for revenge. The Barnsley lads were not ready to leave town themselves and shook off the police before taking over a pub down by the river. The Town mob that night was fucking massive – the gas attack had really wound people up. Again the pub was steamed. It was one hell of a ruck, as over £2,000 of damage was caused to the pub. That's twice they have come down now, so fair play. Maybe it's time we took it to them.

Leeds United find themselves surrounded by much closer and more obvious rivals than those from over the Pennines, yet they regard these teams as we would a spot on our backside. It's irritating and you wish it wasn't present, but you know it's nothing serious and in a few days you will have forgotten it ever existed. Steve A. gives a brief insight into the spots that plague the top side in Yorkshire.

### SO YOU HATE LEEDS? BIG DEAL

There are a few teams that claim to despise Leeds with the same passion and gut-wrenching hatred that we reserve for the scum from the poor county lying across the hills. For them, we are the enemy, yet contrary to what these sad, sad souls believe, we at Leeds don't give them a second thought, as they are worthless nothings. This only frustrates them more, and as they realise their feelings go totally ignored, the resentment grows and festers inside. Still, never mind. The likes of Bradford and Huddersfield would love Leeds to hate them, as they feel it would somehow give them some kind of meaning, a useless kind of importance. It's heart-breaking, really. Let me give you a brief outline of how we view these lesser people.

**Bradford City**: Geographically our local rivals, these poor nobodies hate Leeds most of all. This hatred is born mainly out of seeing 90 per cent of the population of their city catching buses and trains to Elland Road on Saturdays rather than going down to their own little toilet of a ground. As a side, they measure success at not being relegated rather than by League Championships, Cup final wins, European glory . . . shall I go on?

**Huddersfield Town**: Sadness itself. Give a team a new ground and promotion from one shit division to the next (wow!) and they get all excited. We visited their new showhouse for a pre-season friendly and what can I say, it's . . . well, new really. During the game, these saddos showed how low some will go by treating us to fine renditions of 'Glory, glory, Man United' and 'Ooh aah, Cantona'. Bizarre, to say the least, as this was not only an obvious admission of their own lack of importance, but for any Yorkshireman to side with anything Lancashire is degrading. I would like all Yorkshiremen to bear this in mind if ever they come across such scum as those Huddersfield supporters that joined in that singing. They are not the kind of men we need in the Democratic Republic that is Yorkshire.

**The two Sheffield clubs**: Wednesday and United are way too busy hating each other really to bother about us. The mentality of wanting to be the top club in Yorkshire's second city seems enough to keep them occupied. Obviously, Wednesday have come to terms with the fact that there is only one team in Yorkshire capable of winning silverware. As for United, well, being second to Wednesday says it all, really. They can both be good to laugh at, though, because they actually think we care.

**Barnsley**: Now this is a bit of a strange one, because most Leeds fans have a soft spot for Barnsley, just like the Man U scummers do for Stockport or Cockneys do for Orient. This, I feel, is about to change somewhat, as Barnsley have now got above themselves. They can no longer be patted on the head or visited for a night out when all the pubs, clubs, cinemas, corner shops, etc are closed. One consolation here is that Barnsley seem to hate everyone else in the area more than us, especially Sheffield Wednesday. At last, another Yorkshire club with a bit of sense.

**York, Rotherham, Doncaster Rovers and Hull City**: What an exciting bunch, eh? In the words of Mavis Wilton, 'I don't really know.' They say they don't like us, but surely they should hate each other, or any other shit team. All these sides suffer from having such a giant casting a shadow over their futile lives, and that must be as difficult for them as they are meaningless to us. Listen, lads, Scarborough must need some excuse for existing. Go on, hate Scarborough.

On a final note, all these teams, and others from further afield, love to sing 'We all hate Leeds and Leeds . . .' as if they invented the song. Well, sorry, people, you may hate us but as far as we are concerned, you lot just happen to fill up the fixture list between the matches with the real scum. Leeds hate one team and one team only, and as for the rest, you are merely pimples waiting to be squeezed.

Altogether, now: 'Who the fuck are Man United . . .?'

Yes, for Leeds, the rivals they hate with a passion are Manchester United. This may not be a truly 'local' derby, but both teams also look upon themselves as being the true representatives of Yorkshire and Lancashire, and you can't get more local than that. Ian S. sent us his thoughts on this intense rivalry:

## ON THE SIXTH DAY...

On the morning of the sixth day, God created football. Come 2.50, he pulled on his white shirt for he was cold, yet pure. At three o'clock, he was done and ready for a cup of Bovril and a pie. At 30 seconds past the hour, the Devil arrived wearing red and tripped the Lord's little footballers up from behind, only to start whingeing that he never touched them. Much flying of fists was to follow and therefore, by 35 seconds past the hour, Leeds United, God's own work, hated Man United, the bile of Beelzebub.

As was to prove itself throughout the ages, it was the Devil's children that were the cause of all trouble, so the Lord dressed Leeds in righteous white, in order that they should be pure and a shining example to all that were to follow. The Devil's spawn were dressed in red, the colour of danger yet a little bit girlie. The Lord truly did great work that day. The Devil's boys were to change their colour in order to confuse the meek and extract their money at least every other week, but the righteous were not fooled, for they knew tossers when they saw them. Referees, though, were fooled, as were those working in television, for they were tossers also. The fatherless one in black would award penalties and free-kicks at will to the Devils in red, while the pundits, unlike the blind man (John's Gospel 9:7), would fail to see.

The Lord, in his wisdom, has moved in a mysterious way. Somehow, within our hearts, it is our mission to find forgiveness and pity those that follow the dark ones. The hymn 'Who the fuck are Man United?' is to be sung, in order that they may somehow find themselves before attending one of their spiritual meetings at the church they call Old Trafford. Fortunately, many of the Devil's followers never find their way to this pit of shame – 98 per cent, apparently. No, the Naughty One tries to reach them through the power of the airwaves and television (and Lord knows, he has that one sewn up all right).

The Devil would like his brainwashed soldiers to take on the rest of the world, for here they have been sussed. When the Reds continually fail playing among their own in the Greed League of Europe, many lost souls will return. For defeat brings darkness to the shirt of evil, as it remains locked in the cupboard never to see light again. Also hiding in the same cupboard will be old Liverpool and Arsenal shirts, from the time when they were giving false testament. For these people are fickle and easily led.

When the day comes for these sad individuals to finally meet their Maker, they will have one final chance to gain salvation. On that day, all the Devil's men will be given the chance to pull on the white shirt of Justice and therefore save themselves from endless re-runs of defeats at the hands of the mighty Galatasaray (!). It brings great comfort to me that such an opportunity will bring itself to all at such a time of suffering. What brings greater comfort is the fact that all those that had previously led a pure existence will be there to see you doing it. Praise the Lord.

For the Manchester clubs, there is, of course, only one derby, and whatever your opinions of Manchester United fans living in Suffolk or beyond, it is a truly local affair. Sadly, the misfortunes of City have robbed football of this tremendous fixture for far too long now. Hopefully, City will soon be up there with the big boys again, if only because we have always believed City supporters to be among the most loyal bands of sufferers in the country.

We received two United fans' rants about City which rather sum the whole thing up. The first is from Andy of Cheshire and the second was sent to us by Phillip from Manchester.

## COME ON CITY, WE'RE WAITING

I'm getting rather bored of hearing Man City fans singing, 'Who the fuck are Man United?' I mean, they may well ask, because we're not on their fixture list. Why not try looking at the top of the Premiership and not the middle of Dickvision One? The song might be of some relevance if the roles were reversed and we were utter shite, but we're not and you are, so shut the fuck up!

Anyway, don't rattle your brains singing such a complicated song, you should be concentrating on finding out who your new manager is this week.

The amount of City fans who don't go to games yet live within throwing distance of the ground is pathetic, and is proof in itself that Man City is a dwarf club pretending to be a giant. Stop singing crap songs about United and sing songs in support of City. The thing is, you don't even need to be a member to get in at Maine Road, so you've no excuse, you sad bastards.

God created Manchester City so that people could exercise their laughter glands and also give 'shit' an accurate definition. I mean, any group of supporters who go 21 years without winning fuck all, claim to be a massive club and talk of themselves in the 'same league' (you fucking wish) as a team who've just completed four League titles in five years must have either taken a stupid amount of hallucinogenic drugs or be on the same thinking plateau as Francis Lee.

The government should make a law that every Manchester City fan has to have immediate surgery to remove their blue-tinted spectacles, and then they should be sent to laboratories for extensive research to find out which planet they come from. Why are NASA spending hundreds of millions of dollars trying to find alien life on Mars, when all they need to do is spend £12 on the gate at Maine Road and see thousands of little Liams and Noels with blue faces and hooves, torturing themselves?

Please, please get promotion, City, so that we can take humiliation to new heights.

## THE SAD MANC

There's a bloke who lives down my road who guarantees me a good laugh every weekend. Every Saturday, without fail, I see him leave his house in his City shirt and go to watch that shit they serve up at Maine Road. The poor fuckwit, he hasn't got the intelligence to work out that his club are crap and have as much chance of making it to the big time as I have of winning the Lottery.

I have tried to convert him, of course. As I walk out to go to Old Trafford (on whatever day it is these days), I always ask him if he wants to come along and see some real football, but he always tells me to fuck off. Still, some people enjoy a bit of pain, don't they, and I know full well that he'll be going in to watch it on Sky anyway. Hopefully, the poor cunt will realise what he's missing one day.

I mean, it can't have been much fun watching your local rivals rule the roost over the last few seasons, can it? Especially while your bunch of has-beens go from joke to joke. At times, I've almost felt sorry for them, if for no other reason than they're so fucking depressing. The only time you ever see a city fan smile is when United lose, and thankfully, that's been rare the last few seasons. The highlight of last season for them was hearing that Cantona had retired. Fuck me – if that was what football was like for me, I'd have slit my wrists years ago!

All this bollocks about 'only City fans come from Manchester' is a joke as well, but they trot it out as if it's some badge of honour: 'I support Manchester City, so I come from Manchester.' Fuck off! All it says to me is that 'I support Manchester City, so I'm a stupid, sad bastard who hasn't got the sense I was born with.'

I mean, look at them, they're a joke and yet they go on

about United as if we're the ones who have consistently let our supporters and the city down for season after season after season . . . Correct me if I'm wrong, but isn't the trophy room at Old Trafford bulging at the seams after the last few seasons? I did hear that when Denis Law retired, he took the key to the trophy cupboard at Maine Road home with him by mistake. He found it last week and sent it back, but no one had realised it was missing.

The latest trick they're trying, in their quest to gain some decent support, is to convince people that it's trendy to support Manchester City. What the fuck is that about? I mean, if I meet a City fan, the last thing I think is, 'Wow! What a trendy bloke!' I just think, 'You sad wanker!' I suppose it all started with the two Gallagher brothers trying to be hard. All that 'We'll save City' shite they came out with might have impressed a few teenage girlies, but anyone with an ounce of brain knew exactly what they were up to. Still, that might explain why most City fans fell for it. Still, anyone whose eyebrows meet in the middle of their foreheads should be kept off the streets anyway, too fucking scary!

If City ever make it back to the top flight, we'll welcome them with open arms at Old Trafford and then we'll take them for the jokes they are, on the pitch and off it. Still, I'm not holding my breath.

# PART SIX
# The League Of Nations

---

# Chapter 11
# Scotland

For England as a nation, our local rivals are obviously Scotland. Although (as football fans only, we must stress) we hate them and they hate us – as was shown during Euro 96 – we covered all of that in a previous book *England, My England*, and so will not discuss it here. What we will do is take a good look at the Scottish game and the whole derby scene north of the border.

Even the most fervent English or Welsh football supporter must acknowledge that the biggest derby fixture in Britain has to be the Glasgow one. No, not Partick Thistle v St Mirren, but Celtic v Rangers. Neither of us have ever been to an 'Old Firm' game and in any case, to most people in England it means nothing as it isn't *our* derby. But even the most ardent, Sweaty-hating Englishman would have to admit that the atmosphere at that game must be like no other you could experience on these shores. So if anyone wants to invite us up and give us tickets, then feel free. Eddy once saw Partick Thistle play Celtic at Firhill. It was raining bucketloads, 0–0 and shit, but at least Thistle played in yellow, black and red.

Strangely, we struggled to obtain any information on either of the Glasgow clubs, and what we did get was sketchy and not worth repeating. However, it was clear that the rivalry between the two clubs is fuelled by a level of bigotry and distrust that is so deep-rooted it beggars belief. Inevitably, that level of hatred spills over into violence and although the clubs and the police seem to have it sorted inside the grounds, numerous people have told us that Glasgow city centre on the night of an Old Firm game could easily be twinned with downtown Beirut.

The start of the 1997–98 season saw two good examples of this. During serious trouble in the city centre following an Old Firm reserve match (!) watched by over 34,000 supporters, two people died; and the Old Firm fixture due to be played at Celtic Park on the Monday after the Princess of Wales's death was called off, not only out of respect but also because it was feared that a number of the Celtic fans would not honour the minute's silence for her. The possible repercussions for the Scottish game would have been considerable.

While supporters of the Glasgow giants are famous for their passion, they are also renowned for their humour and we did receive one letter from a Celtic fan which gave us a good giggle. Little Ronnie wrote to tell us of his concern for his children and the people of Scotland, Europe and the world.

## THE POWER OF TELEVISION

Just the other day, I had taken the wife and kids to the seaside for a much-needed day away from the drudgery of the city. I have always looked upon Ayr as being a safe place, a place to relax and let the kids enjoy a little bit of freedom as they play on the beach. But sadly, those days appear to be over. As I sat on the beach with my family, I suddenly noticed in the distance, moving towards us quite slowly and with almost neanderthal-like move-ments, a group – no, a pack – of individuals. They were behaving in a manner void of all social graces and self-respect. Quickly I gathered the children.

My fellow human beings cleared a path; it was horrible. They ranged in ages from as young as seven up to 70 years old – and all, yes, every one of these poor people, wore blue-and-white shirts, the colours of sadness. As the area within 50 yards of them cleared of all sane people, I looked in vain for their helper. Surely the care-in-the-community system couldn't have released a whole family onto the unsuspecting public! Thankfully, this group had identified themselves by their lack of decorum and dress sense, giving everyone else fair warning. When things are not going too well, they wouldn't be seen dead in such clothes, as they try to blend in with the rest of society or just stay in.

Luckily, I can spot them a mile off. I have seen them before at the airport up the road. (You know they are there because when the aeroplane engine stops, the whining continues.) I have met many during my time, all lifelong cases. Many showed early signs by following football teams south of the border, mainly between the period of 1979 and 1986. Then, they would wear the red shirts of Liverpool, or the claret of the Villa and once even a different blue worn by Everton fans, all in a vain search for glory. Terribly sad. Since 1989, the problem has grown up here in Scotland. It is, unfortunately, a sign of the times that these people have been allowed out onto the streets, affecting the lives of the ordinary citizen.

I fear for my children and honestly believe that the police should be allowed to give decent folk the name and address of any such individual who is about to move into the area. I once knew of a small child whose life was ruined by these people. He had been convinced that blue was the colour to wear. So much so that one day, he went to school dressed in the full kit. At that age, kids know no different and the poor child was subjected to laughter and ridicule for the rest of the day. He couldn't wait to be released from his torture and, on returning home, locked himself in the bathroom for the next 10 days. The isolation did him the world of good, as now he follows Queen of the South and is a top-notch plumber to boot.

Many of these individuals dream that one day they will be able to take on the rest of Europe. It is forcefed to them at their meeting place that they are good people and that they have the capability. I was once watching *Kilroy* where a family told the story of the son they had lost many years back. They spoke of how he was once a bright, intelligent boy, willing to assist others. Then one day, he changed. He had become arrogant, conceited and self-centred. The little shit. They couldn't understand what had happened and they decided, in a frantic search for the truth, that one Saturday afternoon they would follow him. As he turned the corner at the end of the road, they first became aware of the problems he was suffering. He had suddenly ducked down a side alley; when he reappeared, he was wearing blue! The mother burst into tears as our grey-haired hero and host of the TV show beckoned the cameras in closer. This was moving television, all right. The father explained that he wanted to see just how far his child had slipped, so they continued to track his movements. Sadly, it was far worse than they had ever feared – he went all the way to Ibrox. They couldn't understand where they had gone wrong. How could they have failed to have seen the danger signs? By now, even Kilroy was breaking up.

The father had then tried to retrieve the boy before he entered the abyss, only to be beaten back by more crazed zombies as his son was taken away, never to be seen again. Now the whole audience were beside themselves as tears flowed down the steps, almost drowning the producer. Then the dashing kingpin of the programme announced that a researcher had braved life and limb in search of their son and here he was, live via satellite. The studio gasped. As the boy sat there flanked by two like-minded heavies, it became clear that the years had taken their toll. He spoke of many things, things forcefed to him by the propaganda machine of Ibrox, such as the standard line of being the best club in Europe. But didn't he realise that this could never be? Now that *the* trophy in Europe had been cheapened by those in charge, he surely had to realise that Celtic would forever remain the only Scottish team to win *the* trophy in its original form. He spoke of breaking all the Scottish football records, but didn't he realise that only the mighty Celtic team of the 1960s and 70s had won nine Championships? Those in blue may well equal and even pass that number, but they will only do it in a two-, maybe three-horse race, and in a much-reduced division. When Celtic won everything on offer, they had to play teams week in, week out, that could really give them a game. Not against teams that were there just to make up the numbers.

As the boy spoke, you could almost see the pain welling up inside him as the realisation of his wasted life suddenly hit home: 'Mum, Dad, I am so sorry for what I have put you through. How can you ever forgive me?'

The two heavies also broke down: 'Mr Kilroy, we have families too, please help. We need help.' The screen went dead as contact was lost, then a picture of Ally McCoist appeared. My boot smashed through the screen before I fell to my knees and prayed for the safe return of the boy and his misguided chums. The television has not been repaired to this day, as the Blues appear to have gained some kind of control within the walls of the broadcasting stations. I, like the poor couple on the show, wish to protect my children from future brainwashing. Now it would seem that they are also prepared to fight us on the beaches.

One thing many supporters from outside Scotland do not realise is that there are actually more than two teams in Glasgow. These other clubs are largely ignored by all and sundry or, worse, patronised. What follows explains everything and is anonymous at the request of the writer.

## *DOWN THE ROAD*

As any Partick Thistle fan will tell you, there's only one team in Glasgow. Traditionally speaking, the Old Firm rivalry between Rangers and Celtic dominates football both in the city and in Scotland as a whole, and that left Thistle to build up a healthy rivalry with another Glasgow club, Clyde. The thing is, though, Clyde no longer play in Glasgow and they are as shite as they have always been, while Thistle have played all their recent football in the Premier League or the First Division, so we're different class nowadays.

Naturally, there's no love lost between Thistle and teams like Airdrie, St Mirren, Clydebank and Falkirk, but the teams I hate most are Rangers and Celtic. I fucking hate everything about them. The Premier League in England might be all about money, but at least there are maybe half-a-dozen teams in with a chance of winning the title. In Scotland, we have a 10-team Premier League, a farcical situation that means that you are either fighting relegation or heading for Europe. You can be bottom of the table, win a few games in a row and the next thing you know, you're pushing for a UEFA Cup place. Rangers have won the last nine titles and there's every chance that they'll make it 10 in a row. In fact, the season's generally over by October as far as the title race is concerned.

Rangers fans think they're better than everybody else, while Celtic fans suffer from a mass persecution complex. Both sets of fans are fucking wankers. One time, there were seven of us hanging about Queens Street station, waiting to see if Falkirk were going to bring through a mob. This tidy firm of Rangers strolled by – they were at home too, that day – and one of them asked who we were. We said Thistle and the cunt started chatting away as if he were our best mate. Asking us who we were playing, wishing us luck and all that shite.

It's as if, 'You're just Thistle – a toy football club.'

When Rangers come to Firhill, they take over our ground. Out of a crowd of, say, 14,000, 10,000 will be Rangers fans. They come into the Thistle parts of the ground, wearing their colours as if they own the fucking park. Club officials don't help, selling tickets outside the ground to Rangers fans for areas designated for Thistle fans. There's rarely any trouble – but as far as I'm concerned, there fucking should be! Thistle should mob up and kick any Rangers fans out of our part of the ground, even if they are just scarfers. We would only have to do it once. It's almost unbelievable that they are allowed to come into the home end anyway, but the police do fuck all and the club just sees pound notes. But if there was a massive off and someone was seriously hurt, then maybe someone would open their eyes and wonder how the situation was allowed to happen in the first place. Personally, I work beside the bastards all week long, so I don't want to have to stand next to them on a Saturday afternoon too.

A referee up here resigned a few seasons ago because he didn't like the new rules being introduced. His last game was Thistle v Rangers and he booked Paul Gascoigne. He admits Gascoigne should have been sent off for a second bookable offence, but didn't show the card as he didn't think the rule was a good one! Fucking Orange bastard! Things like that cost us points, and when the division is so small, it's the difference between survival and relegation.

Ibrox is a better ground than Parkhead, though. Walking to Parkhead along the London Road can be a daunting experience, especially if you don't have the numbers to put on a real show. Colours are a no-no these days anyway, but they aren't even to be recommended for scarfers walking to the ground from the city centre. It's not that Celtic have a decent mob, because they don't – for a few seasons, a lot of Celtic casuals actually backed us up because they were made so unwelcome by their own fans – but there are always pockets of blokes wanting to have a go. Mostly neds who throw Irn Bru bottles and think they're hard men because they carry a blade.

Inside the ground, it's like being Christians in a lions' den. Fifty thousand Celtic fans create some noise, and you're stuck in the corner of the ground anyway with maybe 2,000 like-minded Thistle fans, most of whom are fucking hopeless cunts anyway. We tend to attract our fair share of the new breed of football fan, dopey students who think it's trendy to follow football because Skinner and Baddiel say so. They don't want to offend anyone, so they support Partick Thistle. Well, they fucking offend me.

When you win there, though, it's incredible. We never win anything trophy-wise, but it can't be far off the feeling you get when you win a cup. You come out the ground and have to make your way through the great unwashed – we tend to think of Celtic fans as mostly unemployable scum – but when you win, it's a classic. You'd think you'd cheated every one of them out of their giro.

Even a small firm can cause a lot of problems for Celtic fans. Chances are you'll only be greeted by a token enemy mob anyway, but the police are so quick to get in among you on their horses. The police up here have been better sussed for years. Like, one time, I went to see Celtic play at Everton and was genuinely surprised by the lack of respect shown to the police by the Everton fans. Up here, they wouldn't take that sort of shite.

You can usually get another go further away from the ground, but only by chance. Celtic fans don't even have phones in their houses, so the chances of arranging anything by mobile are zilch! But a win and a few lessons dished out to silly wee firms who think they are hard because they come from some no-hope housing scheme is where it's at.

I'm not into trouble anymore, but fair play to those who continue to fight for the Jags.

* * *

If you thought that sharing the same city as your rivals was bad enough, then just imagine having to live virtually next door to them. Such a situation would seem to be a certain recipe for disaster, but somehow the supporters of Dundee and Dundee United have, despite living within spitting distance of each other, managed to live in perfect harmony. Well, almost.

N. and R. provide a brief outline of the relationship the two sets of fans have with each other.

## DARK-BLUE TANGERINES

For the benefit of anyone blissfully unaware of the reversal in fortunes of the two senior clubs in Dundee, here is a brief summary of what has happened to the Dark Blues of Dundee and the Tangerines of United.

Back in the 1961–62 season, Dundee boasted one of the finest post-war squads north of the border. That season they won the League Championship and the following year reached the dizzy heights of the European Cup semi-finals (Rangers fans, take note!). United, on the other hand, had always been seen as the poor relations of the city, living in the shadow of their illustrious neighbours, but things were to change. Following the appointment of former Dundee favourite Jim McLean at United, the team from Tannadice first caught up then raced past their neighbours, and to this day, they have never looked back. In 1983, they lifted the Premier League title. Adding insult to injury, the match that clinched the Championship took place at Dens Park, the home of Dundee. Cup wins and a UEFA Cup final appearance have seen to it that it's been a pretty one-sided affair as far as bringing success to the city is concerned.

The good ship Dundee FC has limped from crisis to crisis and the voyage has almost emulated that of the *Titanic*. Crowds have dipped to below 1,500 on many occasions, as the fans have seen their star players sold with monotonous regularity in order to keep the club afloat. In the face of such a bleak scenario, there have been few opportunities for the Dundee fans to celebrate their triumphs (lest we forget the B & Q Centenary Cup win of 1990–91, or the disasters of United). There are, however, three particular exceptions that spring to mind.

1. At the end of the 1992–93 season, Jim McLean announced his resignation as manager of United in order to concentrate on his duties as chairman. After much panic, the Tannadice outfit appointed Ivan Golac as their new manager. Oops! During the Croat's 18-month stewardship, the Dark Blues' on- and off-park blunders became secondary to the farcical goings-on across the road at United. Golac and McLean held public slanging matches as Ivan's training methods were brought into question. McLean seemed to take great exception to the fact that, rather than working hard on the training ground, Golac was taking the players for days out, where they would drink tea and walk in the park admiring the daisies! Amazingly, the team still went on to win the Scottish Cup during his first season in charge, but the league form slumped and the Croat was sacked. His successor, Billy Kirkwood, couldn't prevent the side from being relegated. Needless to say, many Dundee fans took a perverse delight in such distractions from the worries that were now part and parcel of life at their own club.

2. In the 1995–96 season, Dundee reached a national cup final for the first time in over 20 years. On the occasion of the Coca-Cola Cup final with Aberdeen, the team disappointed before finally losing 2–0, but the excitement and elation among the Dundee faithful was a joy to behold. The highlight for many was once again being able to hold our heads up high and singing, 'There's only one team in Dundee . . .', a song usually sung by the Tangerine fans and directed at us. Well, on 26 November 1995 we were happy to agree with them, as

all the Dark Blues were having a ball down at Hampden.

And finally, 3. The 1996–97 season saw the 'Dee put together another impressive Coca-Cola Cup run, this time making it to the semi-final stage. In the process, they had overcome two Premier League teams: Aberdeen and, wait for it . . . Dundee United. At Tannadice, as well. That game was an epic encounter in which Dundee, the clear underdogs, won 4–2 on penalties following a 2–2 draw. Ex-United hero Billy Thompson was in goal for us that night, and it was Billy who saved the two vital spot-kicks to send us through. This all too rare opportunity to paint the town Dark Blue assumed even greater significance when, just days later, the United manager Billy Kirkwood was sacked. Our victory was seen as the final nail in the managerial coffin.

Unfortunately, the nail was to fly out again as United appointed Jim McLean's brother, Tommy, as their new man in charge. Within a few months, he had transformed the team from bottom of the table no-hopers into a side that clinched a UEFA Cup place. Turd!

Amazingly, the two sets of supporters seem to get on remarkably well. Many families find club loyalties split down the middle, something that probably stems from way back in the 1940s and 50s when many would watch either side's home games. Transportation at the time was nowhere near as easy as it is today, and a trip just up the road to watch top-class football was always going to come out ahead of a long, tiring journey to another part of the country. Unlike other cities, Dundee doesn't suffer from the kind of sectarianism that more often than not breeds violence. The closest thing you get to an Orange Walk in Dundee is when a United player gets sent off.

It would be foolish to say that there is never any violence when the two meet, as there will always be a few hotheads at any game and the passion is as strong here as it is anywhere. But while the monogamy of certain players' wives or partners may well be questioned, I am

glad to say that 'violence' and 'the Dundee Derby' are
not words that sit closely together.

All that sounds like the perfect inter-club supporter relationship, the kind of relationship that, if we could all come together
and embrace it, would make going to football the safest family
day out on earth. While this unique coming together of rival
fans is a credit to the city of Dundee, there is also a darker
side that sits uncomfortably alongside it. Just as those
supporters interested only in events on the pitch happily
tolerate each other, so those from either club wishing to add a
little violence to their day have also, amazingly, formed
themselves into one fighting firm.

By joining forces as the Dundee Utility Crew (DUC), they
have formed themselves into one of the top firms in Scotland.
Just why and how the two have come together is hard to define,
but the most likely reason would be that, on their own, each
would almost certainly struggle against the likes of Aberdeen
or Hibernian. The weight of numbers that Rangers or Celtic
can always rely on would also be too much for them indi-
vidually, whereas together they will put up decent opposition
and often come out on top. It is also fairly well documented
that the DUC have forged very strong links with the Stoke
City firm the Naughty Forty, and many were tracked and
stopped by the police as recently as 1996 while making the
journey south to join up with the Stoke firm as they headed
for a meeting with Millwall in London.

At home, the DUC will come together and travel under the
banner of the city rather than that of either team. Trips to
Glasgow or Edinburgh will often see a large crew travel to
take on the opposing club, and therefore the city. However,
club loyalties often dictate that many will just find a bar rather
than attend the match, before forming up again afterwards to
take on the lads from the local club.

For the Dundee Utility, the biggest test comes in the shape
of arguably the best known of all the Scottish firms, the
Aberdeen Soccer Casuals (ASC), and when the two mobs run

into each other, there will inevitably be trouble. The two accounts that follow were both supplied by D. from Dundee:

## A PURE FLUKE

A couple of seasons ago, due to the football intelligence officers in Dundee being complete wankers and pissing us all off, we decided to play a little trick on the thick tossers.

We invented a story about Dundee and Dundee United casuals arranging a really big off with each other after the derby match between the two teams that coming Saturday. This was total shite, of course, as we're all really the same mob, but try telling that to the coppers. They haven't got a clue. We printed up a few newsletters stating that this so-called off would take place after the game on the outskirts of the city, and left some of them in a few city-centre pubs, hoping that the police would get hold of one.

Within a few days, one of our lads was stopped by the police and told that if he or any of his casual bastard mates caused any trouble on Saturday, they would be arrested. It was then that we knew that they had fallen for it hook, line and sinker.

Come the day of the match, all the United and Dundee lads were having a piss-up together and we were getting loads of reports back about how all the outlying areas were swarming with coppers. But everything passed off peacefully, as we knew it would.

By around seven o'clock that night, there were around 40 of us in our local, having a good-natured bit of Dundee v Dundee United argument, when one of the Under-Fives [Dundee's younger hooligan firm] came running into the pub and told us that a bus-load of Aberdeen were sitting just down the road. Apparently, their match with Rangers had been abandoned due to the weather and they had come into Dundee on the piss, hoping to get hold of a few of our lads and turn them over. This Under-Five was on his way for a bag of chips when around 10 of their lads came out of a pub and chased him up the road.

After hearing this, everyone steamed out of the boozer on their way to get an off with these sneaky ASC bastards. When we turned into the street their boozer was in, they were already on their way out of the pub and so we all just steamed into them. Magic! In the chaos that followed, the ASC in the street tried to do a runner back into the boozer, while those still inside tried to get out to us. Due to this 'mix-up', we were able to knock seven shades of shit out of them, but after a couple of minutes, the coppers appeared and, having got a result, we fucked off. The Aberdeen lads eventually left the pub and started running after us, as if it were them and not the coppers moving us back up the road. When we saw what they were up to, we turned round and steamed them again, but more police arrived and as is always the case, they tried to nick the local lads. We all got away from them, though, thinking that was the end of our night's fun.

But much to my surprise, things went off again. Somehow, the police let around 30 of them slip away and they decided to slip into the city centre for a pint. As luck would have it, there were 10 or 12 of us sitting in this pub, hiding from the Bill, when they came strolling in as if they owned the fucking place. About five of them had made it through the door when one of them looked over, saw us and screamed, 'Dundee!' Knowing that we'd have problems if they all got in, we ran at them and hit them with chairs, bottles, glasses and anything else we could get hold of. It seemed to work, as the rest backed away from the door and after about 30 seconds, the police came screaming down the road. They were already severely pissed off at the day's events and so they grabbed hold of these lads and put them on their coach back to Aberdeen.

We stayed out on the piss for the night, having a laugh

thinking about the day's unexpected events. We heard on the grapevine a few days later that the police were going mental, and that they believed that it was all pre-planned and that the newsletter had been put out to put them off the scent. But it was really all just down to coincidence and, as far as we were concerned, good luck. After all, it isn't every day you put one over on the police *and* your rivals, is it?

## *AT HOME*

With Dundee being in the First Division, the lads don't see a lot of action at their league games, due to the poor standard of opposition. St Johnstone and the 'Fifers' aren't worth getting out of bed for. At best, they'll appear with a handful of lads inside Dens Park, shooting their mouths off, knowing their buses are handily-placed right outside the end to get them away safely. What with that, and the fact that the Bill swarm all over the area due to the reputation of the Dundee casuals, trouble is kept down to a minimum. All this was to change, however, when the draw for the 1996–97 season League Cup quarter-finals was made: Aberdeen were coming to Dens Park. We were all over the moon, to say the least.

By the following Saturday, every good lad had been talking about it and it was obvious that everyone was really up for this one. For Dundee Utility, this was the cup final, never mind a quarter-final.

We got in touch with our ASC counterparts, who informed us that they were definitely showing, with 30 excellent lads. We knew that this was crap and they would bring more like 70. Every casual knows that the opposition always gives you a smaller number, just as they will never give you their travel plans, so that they can catch you off guard. It's all part of the game.

When we had played them in the final of the same competition at Hampden a year earlier, about 80 Dundee, together with about 30 Stoke City Fenton lads, had had a mental scrap with about 100–150 Aberdeen, together with a few Tottenham lads. The Old Bill had just about managed to get between them and stop a full-scale riot taking place, and although neither side had really got a result, it was obvious that this was going to be a big one. With that in mind, and the fact that it was a Tuesday night match, a six o'clock meet was arranged.

On the night, after our scouts had come back with nothing to report, the 40–50 lads we had in the boozer decided to check out the away end, to make sure we didn't miss out on the opportunity to attack the sheep-shaggers. But to our dismay, they were nowhere to be found. With the Bill by now on our tails, we just made our way into the home end.

We were all sat behind the goal and as kick-off time approached, we saw their main mob come into the ground with about 60–70 lads. At least we knew now that they had turned up.

In what was a really cracking cup tie, the scores stayed level at 1–1 until the 90th minute when Jim Hamilton scored one of the best goals seen at Dens for many years. That was it, the lads went fucking mental. We ran onto the pitch, congratulating the players and then only seconds later, in one spontaneous burst, we were charging up the pitch towards the Aberdeen lads behind the goal, offering them a go on the pitch. But they bottled it, pretending they couldn't get over the knee-high wall surrounding the track. Eventually, the police rounded us up and got us off the park, thinking that it would put a stop to the problems. As if!

Next thing we knew, Aberdeen appeared at the segregation fence, mouthing off like fuck. That was it. The lads started battering away at the gate so that we could get into the sheep-shaggers' end, and with about 20 of us at least halfway up the fence, the coppers freaked. They started baton-charging the two mobs, which then resulted in running battles between the police and two sets of casuals. What a laugh!

When the final whistle went, well into injury time, the atmosphere was totally electric. Nothing was going to stop us getting our off with the sheep-shaggers, who, it has to be said, were looking mightily pissed off about their 2–1 defeat and pitch humiliation. They were well up for it as well.

We made our way out of the ground and down to the bus park and, much to our delight, saw about 10 of our lads taking a load of mouth off some Aberdeen casuals. So we just steamed them. After a few minutes of what was turning into a mental scrap, the police appeared with dogs, riot gear and everything else you could think of, and broke it all up. Despite our attempts to get at the sheep, the Bill pushed us down the road and escorted us to our locals. Once we were in the boozer, with no one having been nicked, we sat down for a few beers and a right good laugh about the night's events. We had got a massive result, what with steaming the full length of the pitch to go at their end. An offer the shitbags never took.

Once again, we should stress that if you took five people from a single incident and asked them to write down exactly what had happened and why, you would get five different answers. The whole thing depends on the individual and their own personal perception of events. This isn't just unique to football – as any traffic policeman will tell you – but as far as football violence is concerned, the whole thing is about pride and reputation, with a little bit of shame and embarrassment thrown in. Never mind the actual facts, no one is going to admit that they were turned over unless it's absolutely unavoidable, and in the safety of your local, even a savage beating can become a 'tactical withdrawal'. The mind is very clever at rubbing out the bad times while boosting up the good.

As proof of this, what follows is the Aberdeen perception of their rivalries and is again anonymous by request. We have no idea which is the more accurate and would certainly not want to speculate. However, what is clear is that this view of events involving Dundee is somewhat different from the ones above.

## ABERDEEN

Of all the derby games in Scotland, obviously Celtic v Rangers and the Edinburgh games stand out from the rest. But let's be honest; they, especially in Glasgow, are all about sectarianism. Grown men singing abuse and fighting about something which happened 300 years ago may create a tense atmosphere but they usually make for boring games, as each side is terrified to lose. The Dundee derby is even more boring still, with poor crowds and not much atmosphere – although, to be fair, the two clubs do have small grounds.

Aberdeen are in the unusual position of having no real 'local' derby. However, in the early-to-mid eighties when Aberdeen, and to a lesser extent Dundee United, started beating the 'Old Firm' of Celtic and Rangers on a regular basis, the games between the Dons and United were dubbed the 'New Firm' derby.

Although there is occasionally trouble at other games, the only really organised hooligan followings of any note in Scotland are at Aberdeen and Hibs. The Aberdeen Casuals are by far the largest group and were also the first, preceding the others, such as Motherwell (believe it or not), by several years. Heavy policing and other factors, such as Heysel and Hillsborough, have meant that things have been on the wane, but more recently, there has been a bit of a resurgence.

Trouble in Aberdeen has usually been minimal, due to the aforementioned heavy policing, and apart from the odd Hibernian mob, it's rare for any club to bring any lads with them. One 'New Firm' derby at Pittodrie which springs to mind was back in the early 1990s. For some reason, United brought a mob up on one of their early service trains and took up residence in a bar just up from the station, without any hindrance from the police.

A small group of Aberdeen had gone down to the bar and a fight broke out, but they were chased off under a hail of bottles. Understandably, the police then arrived in force and the United fans were moved off towards the ground, thinking that they were invincible. By this time, the main body of the Aberdeen Casuals had regrouped and were obviously furious at this affront – but they were also resigned to the fact that, because of the police presence, they wouldn't be able to get near United again that day.

However, a couple of hours after the game, when the main bulk of the police presence had moved back from the city centre to police headquarters, one of our younger lads came into the bar and informed us that the same group of United had managed to stay on in a bar near the station. They were obviously under the impression that they had been on a successful foray up north, but we were off to show them that they were wrong.

The Schooner Bar, where they were holed up, is on the corner of a block of buildings leading up to the station and has two entrances, with windows looking out onto the street. With around 40 lads marching down the street towards the bar, we were surprised at the lack of any police presence but decided to split into two groups, one of which had to walk past the front of the bar where the Dundee fans started jeering and laughing as they looked out. However, at the same time, the other 20 of us had sneaked into the side entrance and we came into the bar behind them unseen and laid into them. The United supporters were completely astonished and most of them ran the only way they could, towards the toilet! There were only one or two that put up any resistance, throwing chairs and the like, and one who took a bit of a kicking near the door. We pulled out as quickly as we had come and, with the sound of sirens ringing in our ears, made it back to our regular pub meeting-place, well pleased with our successful revenge and at their pitiful performance.

A couple of seasons later, they again managed to bring a mob to Pittodrie and again managed to stay on after the game, drinking in a bar along the harbour. Realising this, we managed to assemble in a bar a few hundred yards along the road from them and now had them trapped, as they would have to pass our bar on their way to the station. A phone call was made to the bar they were in, telling them where we were and, if they wanted it, to leave at a set time, after the police would have been heading off after a 'quiet' day's work. Instead, they phoned the police, explained their predicament and were driven to the station in a fleet of police vans! That says it all.

The ASC firm became famous among hooligan groups in England as the one which embraced the 'casual' movement more enthusiastically than any other, despite being a few years behind their English counterparts in taking up the trend. It became such a part of their image that they would often ridicule their opposition by sending out leaflets that referred as much to their lack of dress sense as their inability to put up a good fight.

For the two of us, too, being a part of the original casual scene was fantastic. We loved being part of a movement that had an up-front, 'couldn't give a fuck' attitude about it, and we have to admit that the sight of the designer labels making their way back into grounds today brings back many memories for us. Some bad, some frightening, but most of them funny.

Much as we enjoyed the movement, however, others were not too impressed with the football casuals. Sam lives on the west coast of Scotland and supports Celtic. After reading what he has to say, you may well come to the same conclusion as we did: what would he know about style? We reckon that his mum probably hoped for a girl and that to compensate, she merely dressed him funny. But he took the trouble to write in and just because we don't agree doesn't mean what he has to say isn't relevant. So here goes:

## I'D RATHER BE A 'GER THAN A CASUAL

Well, well, it's back, the rebirth of the football casual. Football, beware; fashion victims, take note; because those lads every girl would be proud to take home to their mum are at it again, and don't they look nice?

Thanks to the media hype, wall-to-wall TV exposure and the celebrity fan, the late-1990s version of this trendy 'hooligan culture' has a head start on the originals, as fashion and football now stand shoulder-to-shoulder. Today, the dressers take their lead from musicians, comedians and the new breed of 'Look at me, I'm hard, I'm a TV celeb' laddo geezers. Even the football stars themselves know how to dress nowadays.

All those Christmas tree supporters with their scarves and replica shirts haven't got a fucking clue, and the skins and the rockers can't be counted on when it kicks off, can they? It's got nothing to do with bottle, has it – if you have the right label and that 'In your face, I am the bollocks, me' attitude, then you're made. You are sorted, my son, part of the groovy gang. Scotland, England and even Wales, 1997, and the return of the football casuals; what complete and utter wankers.

Oh, how we laughed at those who took their 'style' from such fashion gurus as Ronnie Corbett, Lennie Bennett and Tarby. The assumption that if you didn't look like Nick Faldo, then you weren't hard enough to be part of the firm, should have been coupled with, 'If you can't run like Alan Wells, you can't join either.' Looking after their gear always appeared to be more important to the casuals than fronting it up for your team. Many found out to their cost that dressing like their Uncle Cyril didn't suddenly turn them into the king of the terraces. Those new Fila trainers that looked 'so cool' came in very handy when they found themselves legging it up the road.

Just why that style was adopted remains one of life's great mysteries. We can only be thankful that such a movement didn't spring up during the glam rock era. Just imagine, hundreds of lads indulging in running battles while wearing lurex jackets weighed down with mirrors, glitter and sequins. All that running around would have played havoc with their make-up, and just how they would have made it through the turnstiles with their Gary Glitter shoulder pads on, we'll never know!

The casuals think it is so clever not wearing the club colours, as they can catch the opposition by surprise. What a load of shite. It certainly helps most of them hide in the shadows when it gets too heavy. It is easy to sneak off and play safe with the mums and dads when you're wearing clothes that would make your granddad look old. Wearing your club colours, home and away, means you are prepared to stand up and be counted. The violence has never gone away, just the casuals who were found out and fucked off into the dance scene. We just carried on using the club colours as our uniform.

There will be many of the old school only too keen to rush off and relive their youth as 'casual' comes around again, but before they fork out a whole month's wages on that latest Stone Island sweater, let us give them one last chance to redeem themselves. I ask all those wannabes out there to try and make a sentence out of the following four words. Victim . . . sad . . . bollocks . . . fashion. Now, fuck off and buy the latest Ibiza '97 dance mix CD and leave the fighting to those of us that want it.

As more Aberdeen supporters, and in particular the ASC, embraced the casual movement, their reputation for putting on a show of force grew. Indeed, in the early-to-mid eighties it became so great that their numbers would often be swelled by lads on scouting missions from England, eager to see just how well-organised the group had become. While the ASC generally welcomed their English visitors – because they would then go back and 'spread the word' – they would draw the line when the number of visitors became too large. Not just to avoid the attentions of the police, but primarily to ensure that the identity of the firm be maintained, rather than have it become known as the ASC plus all-comers.

One of their major battles came when they ambushed the Motherwell firm, the Saturday Service, at a home game in 1985. Despite the fact that the Motherwell mob was much smaller than that of Aberdeen, there had been a long-running feud between the two that had led to many previous confrontations. The Motherwell firm had forged a reputation for picking off smaller groups of fans travelling through Glasgow, and over the years they had scored many victories over Aberdeen's younger firm, the Aberdeen Under-Fives, much to the annoyance of the older casuals. However, the ASC had taken the home end at Motherwell's Fir Park on two occasions and clearly had the upper hand on their rivals. Now the ASC planned to use this fixture to settle things once and for all.

It seemed that as the day came, every hooligan within 50 miles was in the city and knew of the plans that had become the worst kept secret north of Brighton. But the police had also heard about the plans and they set out to smash the firm once and for all and catch the ringleaders. In the end, it was the police who were successful, as the plans for the battle backfired and everything came down on the ASC. The police operation was a complete success, with 47 fans arrested and large-scale violence avoided. Meanwhile, the Motherwell firm were rounded up and escorted back to the station before being put on the next train south. Their anger at missing the game, and the expected off, led to them disembarking at Dundee and taking on the locals there.

The big two clubs in Scotland, Rangers and Celtic, surprisingly don't have the kind of firms you might expect. Obviously, when the Old Firm meet they come out in numbers and, given the opportunity, will indulge in violence throughout the city, but for other games they are mostly quiet, unless something is pre-planned. This could be put down to the lack of opposition they usually face, although Aberdeen, the DUC and Hibs have all taken the fight to Glasgow many times, and even won occasionally. The demand for tickets at both Rangers and Celtic has also had a dramatic effect on their hooligans, as the threat of being banned from the ground, or from owning a season ticket, is a very real one. Unlike most clubs, Rangers and Celtic have the luxury of a waiting list for season tickets, and the loss of one individual means nothing to the club. It also seems to be the case that those hooligans who do follow Rangers and Celtic tend to be older than those from other firms in Scotland, and as the casual movement of the early 1980s did tend to attract the younger lads, it therefore didn't catch on so well at Ibrox and Celtic Park.

Along the M8 in Edinburgh, the Hibernian firm, the Capital City Service (CCS) pit themselves against the lads that follow Heart of Midlothian under the name of the Casual Soccer Firm (CSF). The Hibs firm are probably the second best-organised hooligan group in Scotland and can boast large numbers when called upon. They, too, have a reputation for standing their ground and being prepared to go to the opposition rather than just fighting on home turf. Strangely, many in the Hearts firm, despite the inclusion of the word 'casual' in their name, have always felt that the wearing of the club colours is important. While most casuals wouldn't wear colours, as the lack of identification makes it easier for them to infiltrate ends and indulge in ambushes, the feeling among the CSF is that if you kick or kicked for Hearts, then you took kicks for Hearts. There is also the belief, mentioned earlier, that if you are not wearing colours, it becomes easy for you to bottle out and blend away in the crowd – a charge often directed at their Hibernian rivals.

The following story was told to us by a lad we met while on a train going to Sheffield one day, and is included here because the guy in question is a Hibs supporter. He asked to be called Squidley for some bizarre reason, as his name was Paul, but that's for him to know why, not us. It details a moment of realisation that was triggered by an event of sickening violence and puts across, far better than we ever could, a simple message: stay out of trouble, mate, the consequences are too great.

## ONE MOMENT OF MADNESS

I have spent many hours in cells, talking over moments like this with other inmates. There are a few that really do get off on the violence. You can see it in their eyes as they relive every detail. The stabbings, glassing some poor sod's face, smashing someone's head in. Every word they spout brings my guilt and remorse closer to the surface and once they have gone back to their own cell, I've been left with the image of that poor kid lying on the floor.

At the time, I just went to the matches because everyone else did. You would get the odd chase and pretend that you had played your part as the hardest 16-year-old in Edinburgh, but mostly we would wait right back, watching the real lads fight it out, before chasing along behind or running away in front. The game with Hearts would always mean trouble. They and Hibs hate each other so badly that even the most sane man would kill his wife if she happened to decide to turn from Green to Maroon. All us lot were Hibees and a big thing then was the casual movement, with all the top clothes. The Hearts fans were way behind the Hibs casuals back then and would wear their colours more. Well, we had spotted these lads in the St James shopping centre who one of our lot had known from a previous school. He said that one of them had always been a right mouthy bastard and that he had always wanted to beat him up. They were trying to look like casuals but a few had Hearts scarves with them. There were about 12 of us and only six of them. Some of our lot said that beating up some Hearts fans would have sounded good to all the older crew, so we followed them.

They soon spotted us and you could tell they were worried. Soon we were right up behind them and kicking at their heels, when the 'mouthy' lad turned around and hit my mate right in the face. Those two started fighting but the rest of them did a runner and seven of us went after them. We caught one lad and really laid into him. He didn't want to fight and had probably never been involved in violence in his life, but still we laid into him. Boot after boot after boot, he was being kicked around like a rag doll. Somehow, I still had hold of the bottle of Irn Bru I had been drinking and when we all finally moved back, I threw the bottle right at his head as he lay there. I was not five feet away and he was not moving. The bottle smashed against his head, making the most frightening cracking noise I've ever heard, then we ran. I remember one of my mates saying, 'Fucking hell, what did you do that for?'

To this day, I can't answer that question. It's the one thing I will never know about myself. I can't begin to explain the feelings I have about that moment, I hate myself for what I did then and it will always haunt me. I don't know what happened to him, but I could easily have given him brain damage or cost him his sight. I don't know and probably never will.

From that day on, I have never considered myself a fighter. I've ended up inside, but never for anything to do with football or violence and whenever I come across trouble, I move as far away as possible. If I could go back and change one thing in my life, then it would be that moment, above all others. If I could meet one person, then it would be him, first to know that he was OK and then to ask him to forgive me.

The account you have just read, and the feelings and opinions expressed by the person involved, are something both of us can clearly identify with. On occasions too numerous to mention, we have been in situations where bottles, glasses, coins and ashtrays were flying through the air, and we have been within spitting distance of fights where good friends of ours have either taken a good hiding themselves or given someone a savage kicking.

For us, it was just a part of it all – the game we called football supporting. And as we have said (and been condemned for it) on many occasions, we loved it. All of it. But it was only when friends of ours, or indeed the two of us, were really threatened or hurt that we ever considered the full implications of our actions. Indeed, it was the only time we ever considered *any* of the implications. The realisation that you could end up in hospital because of a bloody football match is a sobering experience, but it is one that hits you like a sledgehammer when you're staring into the eyes of someone holding a knife who has hate in their eyes and who really wants to hurt *you*. Not your mate, or someone you don't even know, but *you*. That's when it becomes different from standing 50 yards away from another group of yobs and hurling insults at each other, because in truth, there's no real threat there. That's all show, 'handbags at 20 paces' stuff. When it's face-to-face, and you know the Old Bill are miles away and it's all down to you and him, that's when it gets really serious. Thankfully, that was something we rarely got involved with. Yes, it is pathetic and yes, it is childish, but tragically, it happens and it happens with a frequency that most people would find astonishing. To justify giving someone a hiding or even taking a good kicking is impossible under any circumstances, but to try to do it under the umbrella of football beggars belief. Yet we have done it ourselves in the past, and we receive letters day in, day out, from people who still do it with total conviction, and that is scary.

But as we have said before, when we started going to football the whole hooligan scene avoided weapons like the plague. If that had not been the case, we would almost certainly never have got involved. Indeed, the increasing use of weaponry at football was one of the major reasons we left the whole scene and became anti-violence in our outlook. But sadly, from what we hear, it is still on the increase and there are far too many people who go to football with a stanley knife in their pocket, or who are willing to throw a bottle at someone's head. That is a frightening fact. There is no justification for it, none at all, because nothing is worth that degree of viciousness – certainly not football. One could argue that if you carry a blade, or any other weapon for that matter, to football – indeed, if you carry a weapon anywhere – then you deserve everything you get, and many people are sympathetic to that viewpoint. But we do wonder if those who carry blades or throw bottles really understand that if they pull it out of their pocket and wave it around or throw it at all, then someone else could die? Do they really understand that if they kill or seriously injure someone, then they will carry that guilt around with them for ever?

When the Scottish hooligan groups follow the national side, it appears that the Aberdeen firm calls all the shots. All rivalries with the Dundee lads and those from Hibs were put aside in the build-up to Euro 96, as the Scottish football hooligans firmed up in order to take on the greatest of all Scottish enemies, England. As was the case with the large English mob, hooligans from almost every club in Scotland travelled south to London, but the followers of the big two were noticeable only for their absence. Celtic were not invited as they are currently seen to have no firm of note, while the Rangers hooligans, who stand behind the Union Jack at most games, would have been almost as unwelcome as the English themselves. Indeed, talk at the time was that Rangers had formed a truce with their Chelsea counterparts in order to avoid any confrontation between the two clubs. However, the planned battle between England and Scotland failed to take place, primarily because the English mobs lacked any kind of leadership or organisation and when it became clear that the only battles the Scots would have were going to be with the police, the truce between the Scottish firms was called off. As frustration grew, the Aberdeen and Hibs fans turned on each other and the Dundee lads joined in.

The Scottish hooligan scene remains an active one both at club and international level. The recent international against Wales at Kilmarnock saw a great deal of trouble, as any Welsh supporter who attended will testify, while at club level, the casual movement is alive and thriving. The young men of Scotland have always been as keen to fight at football as their English buddies and from what we see and hear, that is something that is unlikely to change in the near future.

# Chapter 12

# Wales

---

Go west, young man, way out west, and you move into deep, darkest Wales. A place where ram-raiding takes on a whole new meaning. For many, football takes on new meaning as well, bringing with it hatreds hard to comprehend. The names of Cardiff, Swansea and Wrexham don't sit high on any honours list, but the passion burning within their supporters is as strong as at any other football club. However, as with many other provincial areas, this passion has led to violence when local rivals meet and it is hardly overstating the case to say that the South Wales clubs, in particular, take this rivalry to levels rarely seen elsewhere. The importance placed on being the biggest fish in a stagnant pond is extraordinary.

'Jack Constable' aired his view on a situation that got completely out of control:

## FALLING IN LOVE WITH YOU

'It's all over now. It's all over, mate.' I couldn't believe it. It was 22 December 1993, 10.10, freezing cold – and to be perfectly honest, I was shit scared.

Since seven o'clock that night, I had witnessed the most violent scenes I had ever seen at a British football match. Sadly, the police had completely lost it and I felt for them.

All night they had struggled against a continuous onslaught of fists, boots, seats, weapons and verbal, and for what? So that Swansea could play Cardiff at football. Surely this wasn't right.

That night is firmly fixed in my mind as a turning point in Welsh football. Things would probably never be the same again. Some Swansea supporters (?) will tell you that it was a culmination of years of frustration; frustration towards the enemy that is Cardiff City. Frustration at the biased reporting of a football team that clings onto a few nights of European glory way back in the sixties and an FA Cup final in 1927. The local media are the ones they blame for the explosion of violence that night, violence born out of frustration. They constantly ignored the likes of Newport County, to the detriment of their League status in the 1980s. They refuse to even acknowledge the achievements that Swansea made in the 1980s and ignore Wrexham, at present the strongest side in Wales. For them, there is only one team in Wales, despite the fact that the team in question have the worst record of all during the last 20 years. Yes, adding it all together, Cardiff are bottom in league positions, bottom in goals scored, points won and, most importantly, bottom in terms of support. Go on, check it out; Cardiff City are bottom of the pile, and don't we know it.

So why the constant praise of Cardiff when the Swans stood proud at the top of what is now the Premier League in 1982? What were Cardiff doing then? Nothing, but the support still went their way as far as the media were concerned. As Swansea fell back, they loved it. It didn't matter that we were still above them, they just loved watching us fall to their level and, boy, did they milk it when we finally got back down there with them. This constant bias meant something had to give – and in 1993, by fuck did it give. Now don't get me wrong, because what happened that night was disgraceful and I have to admit that for the first and only time I felt ashamed at being a Swansea fan, but let me set the scene so that you can judge for yourself.

It's 6.45pm and I am sitting in the car on the trunk road into Cardiff, about a mile from the shed they call home. There has been an accident and I curse the driver involved. Later, I found out that a lorry driver lost his life. It's raining, windy and cold. Me and a mate had decided on the spur of the moment to go to the game. We expected trouble and had felt uneasy about travelling to the match from Bath, as it meant we wouldn't be travelling with the main bulk of the Swans support, but this was, after all, the most important match of the season. We had to be there. The accident, Christmas shoppers and those making their way to the match had led to a massive tailback and we finally arrived at the ground for 7pm. I was later to learn that the attendance was recorded at 9,000, some 4,000 down on the attendance for the Autoglass Trophy the previous year. It was also reported that the police had only expected between 800–1,000 Swansea fans, but by 7.15 some 2,500 Swans had swelled the crowd. Unfortunately, not all the Swansea fans were in the same part of the stadium. Outside, all sorts of mayhem was going on and a large group of Swansea had attacked Cardiff fans queuing to get into the seats. The sirens were blaring and the police on foot and horseback steamed in. What stayed with me was the fact that they hit out big time with batons but the Swansea lads stood their ground and fought them off. There was an anger I had never witnessed before, pure hatred.

Once in the ground, I heard stories of pubs smashed up and fights all over the place. There were many faces I'd never seen before, bloodied and excited. Some fans had taken Union Jacks and Ulster flags to taunt the Cardiff 'Bob Bank', renowned for their hatred of all things British. It worked. To our left, a large number of Cardiff came across the seats at the main body of the Swansea lads. They looked mental. The noise was deafening and as the two clashed, I was about to witness the worst battle I've ever seen. Seats flew through the air, hitting anyone, as they met, fighting hand-to-hand. It was unbelievable. It went on and on. The police horses came across the pitch, trying to keep the fans apart, but fighting was going on in other parts of the ground as well and they did their best to cope. There were Swans in the Bob Bank, Cardiff in the Swansea section. People often describe things as being like 'World War Three' – well, that is the only way you could have explained the scene to anyone. If some soldiers had appeared then I wouldn't have been surprised, as I could see nothing else stopping the chaos.

It was clear that the violence had been pre-arranged. That would explain the large following, as Swansea had decided to go for it in a big way. There were people with videos filming the whole thing and within days, copies were available in the local pubs and clubs for all to own. 'Swansea's night of glory', I think the title was. I think not.

I watched most of the action scared out of my life, fearful of being an easy target for the police to arrest, as is so often the case when the real lads are at it. Yes, I was frightened before, I thought I could handle most things. Yes, I was sad; a victory from the players was far more important, but we lost 1–0; and yes, I had witnessed the last fixture where both sets of fans were to be made welcome. Since that night, the derby fixture has been a farce, open only to the fans of the home side. The hooligans have not only killed themselves, as now they have no arena to fight in, but they have killed us as well. How I would have loved to have seen the 3–1 win at Ninian Park last season, but I remain denied.

The one question that hangs in the minds of many Swansea fans is why the ban was only introduced after the Swansea fans took the fight to Cardiff? Did the media and all connected to Cardiff suddenly have enough evidence to lay the blame squarely at Swansea and their so-called supporters? Cardiff fans had rioted at the Vetch many times, but no such action was taken then. There were many events that led to the violence that night and it is true there is a hatred down here hard for the outsider to understand. Much of that anger has come from constantly being named second-best, constantly being put down at the expense of inferior opposition. The media fed the fire that caught light that night. The newspapers, the television and radio all, yes all, played their part. They still don't realise that their constant support for a shit football team and its so-called followers at the expense of the majority breeds anger, and that anger leads us to the vicious circle that is the football violence that has marred this fixture for way too long.

Some may well ask whether the fixture is worth it, whether football is worth it? Well, let me explain. There have been plenty of times when I felt like giving it up. I have honestly tried to walk away and get into something else less financially and mentally draining than following a side kicking around at the bottom of this star-studded game we all love. I have tried, but I can't. When the North Bank booms out the old Elvis song 'When fools rush in . . .' across the Mumbles Bay, every hair on my body stands on end. That is why I can't give it up, because, you see, it's in my blood and now in my children's blood also. To them, I can only apologise and hope that some day, they get to see the Swans defeat the enemy. Only then may they begin to understand that yes, of course it's worth it.

# Chapter 13
# Northern Ireland

The backwater of British football, as far as the rest of us are concerned, is the province of Northern Ireland. Once boasting a set-up consisting of over 50 well-supported teams, the domestic league is now a shadow of its former self. During the more successful days, many teams from the province gained recognition in European competitions, reaching the quarter-final stages on various occasions only to be knocked out by the odd goal or on the away-goals rule. Now, the story is very different as religious differences and sectarian violence, rather than local rivalry, have led to an ailing, one-dimensional league, mainly due to the fact that two of the larger teams, Belfast Celtic and Derry City, are no longer part of it. Both teams were well-supported by the Catholic working classes – and therein lay the problem.

Belfast Celtic were based in the west of the city, a predominantly Catholic area. Their main rivals were Glentoran from the east of the city and Linfield to the south, both of them known for their strong Protestant support. When Celtic met either of these sides, violence was never too far away and on one occasion, a player had his leg broken by rioting Linfield fans. The player in question was a Protestant; whether he was singled out for playing for a Catholic team or whether he was just unlucky is unclear. As the violence escalated, Belfast Celtic took the decision to leave the league, a situation that was seen as comparable to Glasgow Celtic quitting the Scottish league on religious grounds.

The second side to depart the league were Derry City, though many saw them as having been forced out rather than taking the decision for themselves. A Catholic side based in Londonderry, where by the end of the 1960s violence was part of everyday life, Derry City were faced with continued disorder in and around their stadium. For the police and the army, many parts of the city were no-go areas, and Derry City's ground lay in one of the most notorious of these, the Bogside. There was no way the authorities could guarantee the safety of visiting supporters whenever matches were played there, so fans travelled at their own risk. As most teams in the province had a largely Protestant following, especially Linfield, who had massive support, trouble was commonplace. The Irish Football Association and the police felt that as the safety of fans was their first responsibility, they had no choice but to expel Derry City from the league, a decision that was to have far-reaching effects, as many other sides pulled out following Derry's departure. Thankfully, after years in the wilderness, Derry City rose again but now play in the Republic's League of Ireland. If ever there was an example of sport meeting politics head-on, then a team from the North having to play in the Republic is surely it.

The departure of Derry meant lower crowds and a change in the nature of terrace rivalry, as the main Catholic team was no longer there as a target. Indeed, only three teams remain in the league that come from largely Catholic towns or areas. As one would expect, the city of Belfast sees the majority of the crowd problems, providing as it does four very active teams.

Linfield are the most successful and best-supported team in the province, with historically a very strong Protestant identity. This traditional link has meant that only recently have Catholic players pulled on the blue jersey. The supporters, thanks to their Unionist leanings, have formed strong links with Glasgow Rangers and Chelsea and display an arrogance that makes them the most disliked club in Northern Ireland (shades of Manchester United). Violence often follows the team on their travels and sheer numbers make them the most feared and untouchable supporters on that side of the sea. One of their most notorious firms have named themselves Section F.

Glentoran are another highly successful team and bitter cross-town rivals of Linfield. Despite being based in the Protestant heartland of east Belfast, the Glens have never shied away from signing Catholics but have had aligned to them a firm with the rather nasty title of the Nazi Casual Army.

Linfield and Glentoran are the only two teams that can match each other for levels of support and that often results in serious crowd trouble when they meet. The most famous incident took place during what became known as the 'Pig and Cock' Cup final, a match that made headlines for all the wrong reasons. Glentoran are known as the 'Pig 'n Hens' and the club emblem is a rooster. Before big matches, it has become a tradition for Glentoran fans to let loose a rooster onto the pitch so it can go walkabout. On this occasion, the gesture was not going to go unchallenged by their rivals and in return, the Linfield supporters let loose a pig painted in the club colours of blue, an action that incensed the Glentoran support. At the final whistle, both sets of fans invaded the pitch after tearing down the fences and using them as weapons. It was one of the bloodiest football-related battles ever seen in the province.

Crusaders are based in the north of the city and despite having a smaller following, due to the importance of Linfield and Glentoran, have enjoyed a high level of success on the pitch.

Cliftonville are a well-supported, relatively successful team based in a Catholic area of north Belfast and draw Catholic support from all over the province. Although Catholics make up the majority of their fan base, they do also have Protestant followers. Their firm, the PCs, also have a history of crowd violence.

Over the years, many smaller firms have sprung up within the league and one team now troubled by such violence are

Portadown. Portadown lies 30 miles south of Belfast and is a bitterly divided town in terms of religious background and belief. Their local rivals are Glenavon, but there is very little trouble among the two sets of fans. Portadown have a far bigger ongoing feud with the predominantly Catholic supporters of Cliftonville to keep them occupied. C. K. provides the details.

## CLIFTONVILLE

With Cliftonville having a strong Catholic background, and my team coming from one of the most notorious towns in the province for religious bigotry and violence, it is hardly surprising that violence finally sparked off between the two sets of fans. Up to then, there had only really been one previous incident between the two sets of supporters and this took place at a cup match in 1979. But on a hot Friday night in September 1990, all that was to change.

The match, at Cliftonville, was played on a Friday night, due to there being a major Loyalist march the following day in Belfast to commemorate the Battle of the Boyne. The troubles in the province were at their height and the march only helped to stoke up the fire. We knew that travelling into the Catholic area of north Belfast was always going to be hostile, but such is the mentality in this part of the world that it only encouraged more into making the journey. All the pubs emptied out and onto the buses, and it did feel good to have safety in numbers for this particular match. I still believe that if the match had been played on the Saturday as normal, then we wouldn't have found ourselves with the situation and anger that still exists today.

My biggest mistake was to be on the first bus that entered the area. All the buses had set off early and this had taken the police by surprise, as they hadn't yet set up the area for our buses to unload us. As we arrived, the driver realised that he would have to go further down the street and turn the bus around before parking up. We got to the end of the road and soon found ourselves to be in the wrong place, as all the Cliftonville fans had already congregated. We were sitting ducks as the pubs and sidestreets emptied and descended on the bus. Every window was put through and they launched bottles, stones and sticks at us. Some of their lads were trying to climb onto the bus through the places where the windows had once been, and they were hitting out with Hurling sticks. We all just lay on the floor, fearing for our lives, as somehow the driver managed to keep the bus moving until the police finally came to the rescue. I still can't believe I survived that attack, but one old man at the front lost an eye. Just for going to a football match!

The police had now cordoned off the rest of the road and kept back the remaining coaches. All our lot had got off and were going mental, as they had seen what had happened to us. This was to prove a terrifying night. Inside the ground, the atmosphere was electric. It is hard to put into words how you feel in a situation like that: scared, angry, frightened, excited, aggressive, all of those. The match was going well for us and we were 2–1 ahead, when one of their players clobbered one of ours and got himself sent off. They went bananas. Amid all the argy-bargy, a lone figure came out of their end and walked up the side track towards our fans. This lad must have been completely mad as under a hail of bottles and stones, he unveiled an Irish tricolour for us all to see. He then pulled out some matches and tried to set fire to one of the Union Jacks displayed by our lot. I swear that if it wasn't for the actions of our keeper and the police, he would have been beaten to death, as some of our supporters ripped the fence down and got at him. He took a terrible beating, but is probably some kind of hero to the supporters of Cliftonville for what he did!

After seeing our fans on the pitch, the home supporters did the same and invaded in numbers, heading straight for us. I even saw stewards joining in the attack; the very people that were supposed to control the crowd were running along with sticks in hand. We were totally out-numbered and there were many of our fans going down injured with blood pouring out of head wounds as missiles rained in on us. The seriousness of the attack led the police to open fire with plastic bullets in order to regain control, and the match was abandoned. Under very heavy security, we somehow managed to get out of the city, but I will never forget that night as long as I live. The sense of unity among our fans remains strong; it was a miracle that no one was killed, and that wasn't going to be forgotten, either.

The return match saw more violence, with their buses getting the same treatment as ours had, but due to the extra security, it was felt that they had got off lightly compared to the welcome we had received. The policing of the matches became heavier, with 'extra early' kick-off times being brought in to good effect. That was until we drew them at home in a Cup quarter-final a few years later. Once again, I felt the same feelings as at the match in 1990. Both teams had massive support with them and within that support, both had many fans intent on violence. The level of hatred was fuelled by sectarian taunting over religious deaths and so-called paramilitary victories, and it only needed the smallest of sparks to set things off. It came in the 91st minute when Cliftonville equalised, sending their supporters into a frenzy. In their obvious delight, some of their fans scaled the fences and ran onto the pitch in order to congratulate their heroes. We all know that there is nothing more annoying than seeing visiting fans on your team's pitch. That, along with having a semi-final place snatched from under our noses, provoked our fans into invading the turf as well, and a mass battle followed. Bottles, bricks, boots, punches, everything. This time we had the numbers and therefore the edge as their fans tried in vain to get back among their own, only to be met with a shower of missiles. The battle ebbed and flowed for some half an hour as the police failed to get on top. Hundreds were engaged in violence in scenes never seen before. As their buses left following the match, they tried to attack a pub away from the ground only to find that it was full of our lads, only too keen to continue the fight. The buses were smashed under a shower of missiles as they tried, finally, to get out of the town. All this took place in 1995 and it was felt that revenge, although a long time coming, had finally been taken for the attack on us in 1990. It was also felt that this wouldn't be the last incident between the two groups.

Until the start of the 1996–97 season, things had been fairly quiet. However, with the situation involving the Orange Order marching at Drumcree turning nasty, it was inevitable that sectarianism would bring out the violent element in the town the next time Cliftonville paid a visit. An incident involving Cliftonville fans at a town just six miles away led to rumours of a planned attack on their buses that would involve more people than just those that go to football. Portadown play at a stadium surrounded by Loyalist housing estates and when they came, the Cliftonville fans were made to feel less than welcome. As their buses approached, they came under attack from missile-throwing gangs of locals as well as football fans. There were people climbing onto the buses in order to stop them from entering the area, and many sat in the roads to block their path. The police did their best to keep the situation under control, but such was the feeling among the local community that they had no choice but to turn around and go home.

As the match progressed, word got to the Cliftonville players as to what had happened to their supporters and friends. Fearful for their own safety, they refused to come out and play the second half. Not for the first time, a match involving the two was forced into abandonment.

Seven years of growing hatred based on religious rather than geographical grounds have left the Irish football authorities and the police with a headache that is going to be very hard to cure. Quite how they can ever achieve this I certainly do not know, but it is highly likely that Belfast Celtic and Derry City may just find themselves in an ever-growing club.

# Chapter 14
# Holland

Now, we know we're stating the bleeding obvious here, but the derby fixture and all that goes with it are not unique to Britain. The one thing that *is* unique to the British game is the level of support that even the smallest of clubs can drag up.

We do not intend to look at every European league, and in fact had always intended to restrict this book to events within these shores. However, in 1996, Dutch football suffered from an event which we simply have to discuss, because it proves that if left unchecked, local rivalries can really get out of hand. Furthermore, it proves conclusively that the game across the Channel is in real danger from the hooligan groups, and both UEFA and FIFA need to be very wary.

In Holland, there are few sides that can claim to have a large support; thankfully, there are fewer still that share the misfortune of having a large hooligan following. The two clubs with the biggest hooligan elements are Ajax and Feyenoord. Everywhere either of these two play, their fans will outnumber the opposition to the extent that they will inevitably overrun their opponents if violence breaks out. There have obviously been occasions when they have been turned over, but the next fixture against the team whose fans have dared to try it on will see all the old hands turn out in order to wreak revenge. The power and fear that these two hooligan groups impart on the Dutch game means that the Ajax v Feyenoord fixture is not just the most important match for both groups of hooligans, but also the most difficult for the Dutch authorities to police.

The following two accounts came from the same Ajax supporter, who will remain nameless because of their content. The originals have in fact been destroyed for the sake of his anonymity and our safety. The letters demonstrate in the most graphic terms just how far things can go wrong. The first will, for many, get the blood running. The second refers to the now infamous hooligan battle that took place in March 1997 in a field near the small town of Beverwijk, just outside Amsterdam, and should make your blood turn cold. To those of you reading this who are still actively involved in football violence: please take note and stop to think about what he has to say, before it's too late.

## THE RAF OF AJAX

I am personally a member of the Red Army F-Side (RAF), the hooligan mob at Ajax Amsterdam. Most of our lads have good jobs and are not racist, as the news say we are. There are some Nazis and drug addicts in our group, but only about 50 out of 400 hooligans are like this. We always get called brain-dead by the news and they call us racist because we sometimes call ourselves the SS. This stands for Super Slopers, which is Dutch for 'Super Demolishers', it doesn't mean Nazi. One of our lads has a job in the government and there are two lawyers, who will not just fight but also defend us when we are in court. In our everyday life, mostly we are all smart individuals. It is only on match day that we go mad.

All Ajax fans hate Feyenoord with a vengeance. I don't know why, but it is the way it is in Holland. I can't explain it, true hate is inexplicable. For one game, we all met in a bar in the centre of Amsterdam. All the old beer bellies were back for this match and I must have been one of the youngest hooligans there. We took a mob of over 500 down for the match; this was a big occasion for Ajax fans. The buses left from six different places in the town so that the police wouldn't get hold of all of us, if any. The man that ran the buses had sent some of his older ones, because he knew we were Ajax fans and half-expected trouble. He was known to a group of our lads and had asked if we would set light to some of the buses for him to collect the insurance! We didn't, because no one felt like walking home from Rotterdam. Apart from us, 1,500 other Ajax fans went to the game by organised travel.

My bus left from the west of the town, and about 10 miles before Rotterdam we met up with the other buses. No one was wearing Ajax colours but some had brought Feyenoord scarves. When we arrived at the stadium, we saw a welcoming committee of over 1,200 of their fans. When we left the buses, some of our lads started singing Feyenoord songs. I didn't like that – I know it was to trick them, but I could never go that low. I would never sing any other team name, only Ajax. Feyenoord are so stupid that they really thought we were part of them, 500 fans they had never seen before! Once we arrived at the stairs that are the entrance to the square, we started running at them and throwing stones and fireworks. Everyone with us had some kind of tool and we were ready for a great ruck, but there wasn't going to be one as the bastards did a runner. What an anti-climax, but what a victory. We were standing in Feyenoord's square, in their town, burning their flag and singing Ajax songs for everyone to hear.

We couldn't wait until they had regrouped, because they had many more numbers than us. They were twice as many, but we were 10 times more crazy and pumped up for a real fight. We then ran towards our pen in the stadium and ran at the stewards. We did not have tickets for the game but the police let us in to avoid more trouble with the Feyenoord supporters. They always think it is better to let us in than guide us back through the town to the buses, when we could make more trouble. Once in the stadium, we sang louder. We sang about running them in their square, which really made them mad. The team also won 5–0. What a day, one I will never forget, and neither will any other F-Sider.

## WHEN THINGS FINALLY GO TOO FAR

Last week, Ajax and Feyenoord fans made an appointment to fight each other, 50 against 50 of the best lads from each club. The fight was to happen in a field north of Amsterdam and was meant to be without weapons, just fists and boots.

The Ajax fans were there waiting and were unarmed, but the cancer-cells from Rotterdam came with over 300 lads and they were armed to the bone. Our mob was totally outnumbered but we could not just run, as they would have done. We defended ourselves against three attacks, but it was too much. So we had to leave. When we looked back, our friend Carlo was still standing there. He was angry, as we all were, but he should have come with us. Then the bastards came with about 20 lads armed with baseball bats and hammers. They surrounded him and beat him to death. Twenty armed lads onto one unarmed lad, FUCKING COWARDS.

The fight was reported on the news all over Holland. Mr and Mrs Average said Carlo got what he deserved. Goddamned bastards, no one deserves to be beaten 20 to 1. When Mr and Mrs Average see a baby seal killed on their televisions, they immediately send a donation to Greenpeace. The way they beat Carlo was as watching a seal being beaten. They say a seal didn't ask for it, but neither does the cow laying on your plate. Carlo never asked for it. It was a meeting that was meant to have no weapons, remember. We should never have expected the shit of Feyenoord to have had the bravery to turn up and face us with even numbers and unarmed. This will now never go away. We can't forget it, never.

Carlo was 35 years old and one of our leaders. He was married and the owner of a hotel. Those bastards that killed him left two kids without a father. Carlo will never be forgotten. Revenge is ours. Carlo, you will never walk alone.

For the record, in September 1997 eight people were jailed by a Dutch court for their role in the above incident, two of them for four years. All were Feyenoord supporters.

# Conclusion

We live in a society in which violence has become a tragic fact of everyday life. Muggings, burglaries, rapes, murders, child abuse, roadrage, the list seems to be endless. Every morning when we pick up the paper from the front doorstep, there is something new, something even more horrific than yesterday, and we skip over it to look at what's on page three because it happens to someone else. Television is no better. It uses violence as entertainment and rams tragedy down our throats to such an extent that we're immune to things which devastate whole countries, killing thousands, even millions of people. Magazines and computer games which glorify violence are on sale everywhere, and while we ignore them because we know that they're not real, the impact they have on our kids goes almost unnoticed. As a father, Dougie knows only too well that the fighting and the karate-kicking antics that go on in the playground at his young son's junior school come from only one place, and that place is television. That's our fault, because as citizens, we should have been aware of what was happening and stopped it before it was too late. But we didn't and now we're stuck with it.

Football hooliganism is an extension of that. It is another form of violence to which society is becoming immune, for the simple reason that it has learned to live with it. And it has

239

learned to live with it because, in the vast majority of cases, those who indulge in it do so only with people of a like mind. The fact that fans fight each other week in, week out, is so glaringly obvious that it hardly warrants a mention in the press anymore. Only when the hooligans hit pubs in which 'normal' supporters are drinking does it become a problem. Society and football have seemingly accepted that things are as good as they ever will be, and to the two of us, that beggars belief. Can we really afford to let things simmer along until they boil over again into another Dublin, another Heysel or worse? Have we really become that complacent? Remember when admitting you were a football fan was only slightly better than saying you were a car thief or a professional mugger? Do you really want to go back to that? More importantly, can the game, with its reliance on City money and a strong image, afford to go back to that? Of course it can't, and yet by refusing to deal with the hooliganism problem, it is running that risk every time a ball is kicked inside a football stadium.

Don't doubt for one second whether what we say is the truth. If you are one of those who has swallowed the football establishment's propaganda and believes that the hooliganism problem has been solved, then please tell us why we still see so many policemen at games and why fans are still segregated. You might also care to explain to us why some pubs near grounds get closed down on match days, why most local derbies are all-ticket, why some games kick-off in the morning, why visiting fans are kept behind after games, why the press panic when England or English clubs travel abroad, why the Home Internationals are still banned, etc, etc. But you know, deep down, that we're right. And we've always been right.

In our books, we have looked at the real reasons for the existence of football hooliganism, as well as how the two of us became involved in it – and why, eventually, we stopped. We have analysed many of the so-called facts about football violence put out by the FA and those academics who study the hooliganism issue, and we have blown them apart. We have examined the role of the police and the media, and looked at the domestic, European and international scene. We have also written about the background behind the London clubs and their violent following. We have done all these things from the perspective of two blokes who once played up a little and who are now anti-violence in every way possible, and we did them because we were sick of reading the utter tripe that was being put out, telling us how and why *we* did what we did. Quite simply, we did it to put the record straight.

But using that experience, we have also put forward our own suggestions as to ways in which the game could adopt a pro-active approach and deal with this problem once and for all. Measures which we – as former hooligans, remember – believe would have a positive effect on the way that supporters behave at games. The time has come to go over it once again, and we do so only in the hope that one day, someone will listen to what we say and finally take our ideas on board. Sadly, we have no reason to be optimistic.

The key is to send a clear message to the hooligan groups that their behaviour will not be tolerated anymore, under any circumstances. The only way to do that is with action, not words. Since they carry on their activities in the name of their club, then those clubs must disown them, as groups and, if convicted, as individuals. Then they must ban them, for life. We know that it's easy for Arsenal or Rangers to ban 30 people, because they will just be replaced by another 30; but the same must go for the likes of Exeter or Hartlepool, no matter what the cost to those clubs in terms of lost revenue. It would send a message to the hooligans that they are not wanted, and it would send another message to the local, decent fans: that the club is working to resolve the problem and the ground is a safe environment to visit. Do that, and hopefully, those who stay away might well come back.

As an extension of that, we believe that the clubs, the FA and the Commission for Racial Equality (CRE) must stop harping on about football grounds being a hotbed of racism, because in our experience, not to mention the experience of almost every football supporter we speak to (of all colours and religions, we should add), it is just not true anymore. Worse than that, it's counter-productive, because what young Asian lad is going to walk into a place which, according to the men in suits, is home to racists who will abuse him? Of course there are clubs which are worse than others, but racism in any form is about bad manners and inside football grounds, those bad manners are usually directed at opposing players who are a danger to their side. That's all. Deal with racist abuse, of course, but we should widen the net to deal with intimidation in all its forms. That includes *all* types of aggressive and abusive chanting, as well as bad behaviour.

The police – hardly our greatest admirers, either – have a difficult job to do at football but they could help themselves a great deal. Just using the weapons already at their disposal would be a start. But they don't, and the hooligans quickly learn what they can get away with and where. For example, at Watford, visiting fans have quite a long walk to the away end. Those of them who can't be bothered simply sneak into the home end late – which also gives them time for a few more pints – and start chanting for the visiting team. They will then get taken around the edge of the pitch to the away end, giving it the biggie as they go. The next season, a few more lads do it; the season after that, a few more. As word spreads through the terrace grapevine, everyone starts to try it. So you soon have plenty of pissed-off Hornets and eventually, it kicks off, just as it did against Spurs a few seasons back. Then, of course, you get Watford supporters arrested and in court for disorder, damaging the good name of the club, all because a few stewards and policemen were too weak to nip a simple problem in the bud. If fans are caught in the wrong end of a ground, they are there for one reason only and should be taken out and held until the game has finished. End of story. If they play up at all, then arrest and charge them. If they're caught on CCTV doing anything they shouldn't, track them down and punish them. The stewards know who they are and where to find them, because most people now sit in the same seat every week. They should use that knowledge and get rid of those who seek to damage football for the rest of us. If they're away fans, send the film to the visiting club and get them to deal with it. The rules are there, use them.

When police forces and clubs start doing that, the hooligan groups will soon get the message. Those who are convicted of a football-related offence in a court of law should be made to report to stations and kept there during matches. If they are told to report and then don't, then charge them again. It really is that simple. If you have two blokes who want to have a fight, get rid of one and the problem has been solved, because you cannot have a decent punch-up by yourself.

The other thing clubs could do is to actually start some kind of dialogue with those of us who walk through the turnstiles. Yes, the disabled are important, as are women, children and the corporate boys with their free tickets, but the fact is that the vast majority of people who pay at the gate are blokes. And yet the opinions of the male supporters are never canvassed, our needs never discussed or pandered to. We know that toilets are vital, catering must be up to scratch and the programme must be value for money, but as blokes, we go to football for fun. We like to stand and sing and shout at those on the pitch, and we should be allowed to do that – but we're not allowed to, in case it upsets everyone else. We accept that the idea of diluting the male-dominated environment to counter the hooligan threat was done in good faith, but it has not worked and, to be honest, it never could. So talk to the blokes, pander to *our* needs and we will respond. With noise, support and atmosphere, and if you do it right, in perfect safety.

Players also have a role to play. After all, it is often their behaviour which starts the crowd off, so they should be told by the FA and their clubs exactly what is expected of them, on and off the pitch. Players need to show supporters that they are committed to their clubs and the local area, not just on the pitch but by their deeds off it. At Watford a few seasons ago, we had a problem with a number of players who refused to move near to the ground. Not next door, just within about a 45-minute drive, but some refused and it pissed off the supporters. When the great god Graham Taylor returned, those who would not make the move were given one last chance and, if they still refused, they were offloaded and quite rightly. Players should be made to visit local schools to encourage kids to play the game and visit the local club. It's very important for the future of the game, and yet there are still clubs where players refuse to do it. Crazy. On the pitch, players have to stop arguing with referees and each other. Stamping, elbowing and spitting are all disgusting, not to mention dangerous, but all of those things go on and it fires up the crowd to the point where anything can happen. Yet at some clubs, it seems these things are almost encouraged. The FA must really start to hammer those who break the rules and then they should hammer the clubs. Not just financially but where it really hurts, by deducting points from clubs who do not conform to a set and expected standard. If the FA started that, we believe many of the problems with players would be solved overnight. But we've said all this before and don't wish to become boring, so we won't be saying it again.

Not everyone who reads this book will be a fan of ours but we can live with that; after all, if you're going to stick your head above the parapet, you have to be prepared to be shot at. But we have been lucky in that with very – and we mean very – few exceptions, everyone we have ever met or who has written to us has been supportive and complimentary of what we have said. For that, we can only offer our humble and heartfelt thanks, for it backs up everything we have ever said or written. The culture of hooliganism and the whole gang-warfare ethos that accompanies it has been explored by us in a way that tells it like it was for us and, judging by the response we have received, how it is and was for others. We have been condemned and criticised by the media for that statement more than any other, but it's the truth. And unlike others who write about the hooliganism issue, we will only write about our own experiences or those of others whom we have met or who have written to us. We don't make it up, we don't dress it up, we just repeat it.

# Conclusion

Could it be that those who condemn or are critical still do not understand? Or is it simply that they have experienced it themselves and are in denial? Have they been the victims of hooliganism at a game and still seethe at the humiliation to such an extent that when something lands on their desk which hits the mark, they exact revenge in the only way they can – through criticism? Or is it something worse?

During the Trafalgar Square riot in the aftermath of the England–Scotland match during Euro 96, a well-respected editor of a very well-respected football magazine came up to us and told us how he had just been throwing bottles at the Scots and what a tremendous buzz he was getting! Did we catch the moment there and get a bit too close to home for comfort? In truth, as we have said on many occasions, we don't really care. Our books sell, as we knew they would, because they're the books *we* would want to read, as blokes who are football fans. If that sounds conceited, it isn't meant to. But we're sick to death of being slagged off by people in the media who refuse to talk to us face-to-face, but sit behind a desk and tell us how *they* know us and our type better than we know ourselves. One letter from a genuine football supporter is worth a thousand reviews to us, because they are the people we write the books for and they are the people whose opinions really matter to us.

Yet we doubt we will write another on the subject of football hooliganism – at least, not for a while. Our aim was always to force the game to accept that it still has a hooligan problem on its hands and get those who run it to deal with the problem head-on – and in that, we have not succeeded as we would have liked to. The game has largely continued to ignore the problem of football hooliganism, while forcing clubs to spend huge amounts of their income policing games, even if very often they simply cannot afford it. That, in itself, borders on criminal.

We have never pretended to have all the answers and yet, as two blokes who openly admit to having been involved in trouble at football back in the 1970s and early 1980s, we believe we have put forward more constructive ideas than any other so-called 'expert' we have ever met, heard or read. Despite this and despite numerous letters to so many official bodies, we remain as frustrated as when we sat down and wrote the first few pages of *Everywhere We Go*. Within all our work, we have always condemned hooliganism in all its forms and those who have taken part in it, including ourselves. 'If people did not fight at football, there would be no problem' is the statement we have used probably more than any other – but the fact remains that they do, and there is, and no one except the two of us seems to give a shit.

Well, so be it. To those who have supported us, be they football fans or even journalists, we say a very humble thanks. To the rest, all we can say is take care. When it all falls apart and the bubble bursts don't say we didn't warn you.

Keep the faith lads, and for the sake of the game, keep out of trouble.

'Up the 'Ornets!'

# Capital Punishment

## Dougie and Eddy Brimson

London is home to some of British football's most notorious hooligans. However, the history of such infamous 'firms' as the ICF, the Headhunters and the Bushwhackers has never been fully documented . . . until now.

From the authors of the bestselling *Everywhere We Go* and *England, My England* comes a remarkable and frank examination of football violence involving the supporters of clubs from the capital. They explain not only how these groups have gained and maintained their reputations, but also why hooligans from other parts of the country see a trip to London as their biggest challenge, and how the system of public transport opens up opportunities for those who wish to fight. Each of the major clubs is studied to assess why some seem to attract a more violent following than others and to explain how different inter-club and inter-regional rivalries have evolved. *Capital Punishment* is an eye-opening study of a problem that refuses to go away.

Reviews for their previous books:

*Everywhere We Go* . . . 'probably the best book ever written on football violence' *Daily Mail*

*England, My England* . . . 'quite simply brilliant!' *Sky Sports Magazine*

**NON-FICTION / SPORT 0 7472 5713 2**

This book would not have been
possible without the help of football supporters
from all over the country.

If you have any views on the contents of this
book or would like to help us with our football-
related research please do not hesitate to
contact us at the address below.
We will add your name to our database
and send you regular questionnaires on
the issues that affect *you*, the
football supporter.

**This is an opportunity to have your say.**

All correspondence will be treated with the
utmost confidentiality.

Please write to:
**Fandom**
**P.O. Box 766, Hemel Hempstead, Herts,**
**HP1 2TU**